PTSD

WHAT EVERYONE NEEDS TO KNOW®

PTSD

WHAT EVERYONE NEEDS TO KNOW®

**BARBARA O. ROTHBAUM
AND
SHEILA A. M. RAUCH**

OXFORD
UNIVERSITY PRESS

Oxford University Press is a department of the University of Oxford. It furthers
the University's objective of excellence in research, scholarship, and education
by publishing worldwide. Oxford is a registered trade mark of Oxford University
Press in the UK and certain other countries.

"What Everyone Needs to Know" is a registered trademark of
Oxford University Press.

Published in the United States of America by Oxford University Press
198 Madison Avenue, New York, NY 10016, United States of America.

Library of Congress Cataloging-in-Publication Data
Names: Rothbaum, Barbara O., author. | Rauch, Sheila A. M., author.
Title: PTSD : what everyone needs to know® / Barbara O. Rothbaum,
Sheila A. M. Rauch.
Description: New York : Oxford University Press, [2020] |
Series: What everyone needs to know® |
Includes bibliographical references and index.
Identifiers: LCCN 2019044918 (print) | LCCN 2019044919 (ebook) |
ISBN 9780190930370 (hardback) | ISBN 9780190930363 (paperback) |
ISBN 9780190930394 (epub)
Subjects: LCSH: Post-traumatic stress disorder.
Classification: LCC RC552.P67 R68 2020 (print) | LCC RC552.P67 (ebook) |
DDC 616.85/21—dc23
LC record available at https://lccn.loc.gov/2019044918
LC ebook record available at https://lccn.loc.gov/2019044919

1 3 5 7 9 8 6 4 2

Paperback printed by LSC Communications, United States of America
Hardbback printed by Bridgeport National Bindery, Inc., United States of America

CONTENTS

Introduction   **1**

   What is trauma?   *1*

   What are some types of traumas?   *2*

   *What are emotional stressors that aren't usually considered to be
traumatic, and why is this so?*   *4*

   Who experiences trauma?   *4*

   What is posttraumatic stress disorder?   *5*

   Why do some people develop PTSD and not others?   *5*

   What are some common traumatic events that can lead to PTSD? *6*

   How long has PTSD existed?   *7*

   What are some treatments for PTSD?   *8*

   Are human beings resilient?   *9*

1 How Do People React to Trauma?   **11**

   What are some common reactions to trauma?   *12*

   What are some risk factors for longer term problems following trauma? *15*

   Can you give some examples?   *16*

   Who is likely to get PTSD and who will be OK?   *21*

   What are common risk factors for trauma-related problems? *22*

   *What is a helpful framework to better understand how we
experience trauma?*   *25*

What is posttraumatic growth?   27

What about physical health or chronic pain following a traumatic event?   28

Is it possible to prevent the harmful effects of trauma?   29

How do thoughts, emotions, and behaviors relate to each other?   29

Does treatment affect the trauma memory?   32

What is good advice following a trauma?   36

2   What Help Is Available to Those Who Have Experienced Trauma?   37

What do rape survivors need immediately after the assault?   38

Cynthia's night at the ER   41

What is interpersonal violence, and what do survivors need?   43

What can you do if you suspect childhood abuse?   45

What about survivors of natural disasters?   47

Who are first responders, and what are their needs?   48

What do military service members and Veterans need?   50

Can you provide an example of a military service member who
experienced a traumatic event?   51

What about burn survivors?   53

What are common needs of trauma survivors?   54

What should you not say to a trauma survivor?   55

What do families of survivors need?   57

How can you help yourself?   59

How can you help others who have survived trauma?   61

How do PTSD sufferers handle the reactions of those who love them?   61

What can survivors tell close friends and family members after a
traumatic experience?   63

Does exercise help?   67

What are other services that aren't actual treatment?   67

Is there such thing as needing to be ready for treatment?   68

How soon after the trauma should a survivor wait to get treatment?   70

What type of early intervention did Lucia receive in the ER?   70

3 What Is PTSD?   75

What are the symptoms of PTSD?   75

What are the DSM and ICD?   82

How can you tell the difference between chronic grief and PTSD?   83

What are some other non-PTSD problems that can develop
after a trauma?   84

What about people who have some symptoms but may not meet the
full diagnostic criteria for PTSD?   91

Does it mean that you are weak if you have PTSD?   92

Isn't PTSD the "war Veterans' disease?"   93

Are there genetic factors that impact PTSD?   93

Are there other risk factors for developing PTSD?   94

What about people who develop PTSD and substance abuse?   96

What are the consequences of having PTSD?   98

How is PTSD diagnosed? Is there a blood test for it?   100

How common is PTSD?   101

What online tools are available for people who want to learn more
about trauma survivors and PTSD?   102

4 What Are the Treatments for PTSD?   105

What kinds of people treat PTSD? How do I know if they are good?   105

What kinds of therapies help PTSD?   106

What is prolonged exposure (PE)?   107

What is cognitive therapy?   114

What is cognitive processing therapy (CPT)?   115

What is eye movement desensitization and reprocessing (EMDR)?   116

What does evidence-based care mean?   118

What about other treatments?   119

What tools or resources are available for people working through
PTSD treatment?   119

What online tools or apps are available for people in treatment
for PTSD?   120

Are there medications for PTSD?   121

What about yoga and other wellness activities?   123

What is sleep hygiene, and why is it important?   123

What does "exposure" mean for a trauma survivor?   126

Has any organization rated treatments for PTSD?   126

Does the PTSD sufferer's preference matter?   127

How can we tell if the treatment is working?   127

What can survivors do if they feel like dropping out of treatment?   129

What about booster sessions?   131

What if treatment didn't work?   131

What about anniversary reactions?   133

Can you provide an example of what treatment would look like?   133

5 How Are Children Impacted by Trauma?   137

Is trauma common in children?   137

How important are caregivers in children's experience of trauma?   139

What about neglect?   140

Jonathan's abusive father   141

Does trauma impact schooling?   142

Do children get depressed or have PTSD after trauma?   143

How are trauma reactions different in children?   144

What should we do after a child has been exposed to a traumatic event?   147

Are there treatments for children with PTSD?   148

How important is it for children to hear repeatedly, "It was not your fault"?   150

Afterword: A Message of Hope and Resources   153

A message of hope   153

How to find a provider   154

PTSD resources   154

Afterword in the Face of the COVID-19 Pandemic   159

INDEX   161

INTRODUCTION

What is trauma?

When we listen to the news or go online, we often hear or read about trauma and traumatic events rocking our world. Some of these events have ripple effects beyond those directly affected, and many events go undocumented, unreported, and often unsaid.

Trauma can happen to anyone at almost any time. More than 2 million people are injured and over 30,000 are killed in car crashes in the United States every year. One in four to five women will be a victim of sexual assault in her lifetime. In 2018 multiple natural disasters occurred in the United States. The #MeToo movement is highlighting how common sexual harassment and assault are, and this movement is encouraging support for survivors.

What makes an event traumatic is that there is usually an injury or the possibility of an injury. It is a physical stress (such as a wound) or an emotional stress (such as fear for one's survival) that impacts our lives. Very often in a trauma, we feel that we or someone we care about could be seriously injured or killed. It is a big event that may change the course of our lives. In this book, we will discuss different types of traumatic events and how such experiences can affect us.

What are some types of traumas?

Sexual trauma

Sexual trauma can take many forms:

- Sexual harassment means hearing unwanted sexual or obscene comments that can make us feel uncomfortable, fearful, or angry. If this harassment happens where we work, then our workplaces can become unwelcoming environments. If it's our supervisor (or another person in power) making these comments, this can create a situation that can lead us to sometimes feel powerless.
- Rape involves penetration—oral, anal, or vaginal—without your permission. If someone is too intoxicated to give her permission or if that person is unconscious, that is also considered rape. We consider rape a crime of aggression using sex as the weapon; it is not sex.
- When sexual contact is by an adult with a minor, this is called childhood sexual abuse.
- Sexual molestation is a term used to describe an adult touching a child sexually or using the child or parts of the child's body to touch an adult sexually. Children cannot consent to any sexual activity with an adult, so any sexual activity involving a child is childhood sexual abuse, even if the child says it is OK.
- The person who forces another person into sexual activity without his or her consent is called a perpetrator.

Nonsexual violence

Violence is another cause of trauma. Rates of gun violence—including mass shootings and hate crimes—are on the rise. Interpersonal violence, which is violence by people against other people, including gun and physical assaults, leads to lasting stress at very high rates. Interpersonal violence can occur between people who are in romantic relationships (either married or unmarried), and when this occurs, it is called domestic violence.

Natural disasters

Natural disasters—like earthquakes, hurricanes, wildfires, mudslides, and tornados—affect millions of people every year. The people most at risk for developing lasting problems following a natural disaster are those who have experienced significant losses such as the death of a loved one, a serious injury, destruction of their home, and being separated from their family, friends, and community.

Military trauma

Military personnel are knowingly put in harm's way. Whether they have volunteered or were drafted, they are at high risk for being exposed to traumatic events. These events can include the same types of events as civilians experience, such as those previously described, but also includes combat trauma. Sometimes this can occur on home soil in training accidents or in attacks, such as terrorist attacks. Military personnel sent to combat zones may encounter an enemy trying to kill them with bullets, bombs, improvised explosive devices, poisonous gas, cutting off supplies to starve them out, or many other deadly means.

First responders/high-exposure professions

Like military service members, first responders, emergency workers, firefighters, and police go toward danger and are exposed to potentially traumatic events at higher rates than the general public. While most of these professionals do not develop lasting emotional problems, a significant minority are haunted by the things they've seen.

*What are emotional stressors that aren't usually considered
to be traumatic, and why is this so?*

Getting a divorce or having a loved one die can be extremely difficult experiences, but these losses are usually not considered to be traumatic. The same is true for getting really sick, going through a difficult financial period, or losing your job or housing. The distinction between these types of stressful events and trauma is that these events do not pose an immediate threat to your physical integrity or to your life. That's not to say that these are not extremely upsetting and disruptive changes to your life that result in fundamental changes to how you see yourself and the world, but the usual results and any treatment after these events are different from what we expect following trauma.

Who experiences trauma?

We constantly hear about people affected by trauma. Soldiers returning from distant wars; survivors of domestic abuse, rape, or other assault; people who have lost their homes to fire or flood; witnesses to crime or shootings; survivors of car crashes; victims of terror and mass shootings such as in Las Vegas, in the American Methodist Episcopal Church in Charleston, South Carolina, and in the Tree of Life Synagogue in Pittsburgh; and refugees from violent homelands—all of these folks, and many others, may experience trauma. Your family members, friends, coworkers, teachers, grocery store clerks, healthcare professionals, car mechanics, or you yourself may be affected by trauma and may experience the aftermath.

Trauma is pervasive, but the strength and resilience of the human spirit is awe-inspiring. Despite high rates of trauma, most trauma survivors recover, and many even thrive after these negative experiences. Newspaper headlines often link war Veterans with trauma, and trauma is certainly a problem in that group, but scientific studies estimate that as many as 70 percent of us will experience a traumatic event in our lifetimes—a huge percentage of people, including both children and adults.

What is posttraumatic stress disorder?

One negative reaction to trauma is posttraumatic stress disorder (PTSD), which is a severe, often chronic, and disabling disorder. PTSD develops in some people following their exposure to a traumatic event involving an actual or threatened injury to themselves or to others. A person with PTSD may have intrusive thoughts, nightmares, and flashbacks of past traumatic events. They may avoid reminders of the trauma, become "hypervigilant," and develop sleep disturbances. In addition, changes in thoughts and mood, and quickly becoming aroused or angry are symptoms of PTSD and may lead to many social, occupational, and interpersonal problems. To be diagnosed with PTSD, a person will have symptoms that have lasted for at least one month. Someone with chronic PTSD is diagnosed when the symptoms have been present for at least three months, and once PTSD has become chronic, it is unlikely to improve without treatment. Both adults and children can develop PTSD, although the symptoms might look a bit different in kids. People with PTSD feel haunted by something that happened to them in their past.

Why do some people develop PTSD and not others?

Not everyone who experiences trauma develops PTSD or has other long-term negative effects. Some people even report a sense of accomplishment and increased confidence and strength following trauma. Many factors determine (a) who will have long-term problems following trauma, (b) who will recover without significant effects, and (c) who will experience posttraumatic growth. These factors include (a) those related to the type of trauma, (b) those related to the person's thoughts and reactions at the time of the trauma and after, (c) biological factors, and (d) how other people react to the trauma and its aftermath, including the person's social support.

The symptoms of PTSD are also part of the natural response to trauma. For example, one study found that 94 percent of survivors of rape developed PTSD symptoms within a week of the assault and that number decreased to 47 percent still experiencing PTSD three months after the assault. Those who do not end up with chronic PTSD continue to improve over time, whereas those who do end up with chronic PTSD get stuck after about one month: They don't get worse, and they don't get better. This finding has led many experts to think of PTSD as a "disorder of extinction," which is explained as follows. Fear and anxiety is a normal response to trauma, and for many survivors, the fear goes away (extinguishes) over time. However, for people who develop PTSD, this fear does not go away, and, instead, it leads to avoiding situations that may remind them of the traumatic experience. However, avoiding situations that remind survivors of the traumatic event, such as not driving following a car crash or not going to the grocery store after being mugged in the parking lot, doesn't allow the survivor to experience that every similar situation is not realistically dangerous. This allows the fear to fester unchecked. While fear is a driving force in PTSD, other emotions such as guilt, sadness, and anger can also add to distress and avoidance in PTSD. There are different theories for how PTSD develops, but experts are certain that avoidance is what keeps PTSD going.

What are some common traumatic events that can lead to PTSD?

As previously noted, chronic PTSD affects almost one half of all rape survivors of all sexes. Other common traumatic events include car crashes, natural disasters, nonsexual assault, terrorism, industrial accidents, fires, combat, hearing about the violent death of a loved one, and almost any event in which survivors thought that they or someone they care about could be killed or seriously injured. PTSD is widespread and is undoubtedly a public health problem.

How long has PTSD existed?

PTSD has existed as long as humans have been humans, but it just wasn't called PTSD. Shakespeare, in *Henry IV*, Part 1, nearly perfectly described the American Psychiatric Association's *Diagnostic and Statistical Manual of Mental Disorders* (DSM) symptoms of PTSD in the observations of Hotspur's wife, Kate, on her husband's behaviors after repeated mortal combat:

> O, my good lord, why are you thus alone?
> For what offence have I this fortnight been
> A banish'd woman from my Harry's bed?
> Tell me, sweet lord, what is't that takes from thee
> Thy stomach, pleasure and thy golden sleep?
> Why dost thou bend thine eyes upon the earth,
> And start so often when thou sit'st alone?
> Why hast thou lost the fresh blood in thy cheeks;
> And given my treasures and my rights of thee
> To thick-eyed musing and curst melancholy?
> In thy faint slumbers I by thee have watch'd,
> And heard thee murmur tales of iron wars;
> ... Of prisoners' ransom and of soldiers slain,
> And all the currents of a heady fight.
> Thy spirit within thee hath been so at war,
> And thus hath so bestirr'd thee in thy sleep,
> That beads of sweat have stood upon thy brow
> Like bubbles in a late-disturbed stream;
> And in thy face strange motions have appear'd,
> Such as we see when men restrain their breath

On some great sudden hest. O, what portents are these?
Some heavy business hath my lord in hand,
And I must know it, else he loves me not.

Until the appearance of PTSD as an official diagnosis in 1980, many of the reports referred to the constellation of symptoms according to the index trauma, as in "traumatic hysteria from railroad injury" and "rape trauma syndrome." During the Civil War, stress reactions were known as "Da Costa syndrome" or "irritable heart." World War I referred to "shell shock," "soldier's heart," or "the effort syndrome." The term "acute combat stress reaction" was used during World War II, as were the synonyms "battle fatigue," "combat exhaustion," or "operational fatigue," among aviation personnel. Finally, in 1980, "posttraumatic stress disorder" became an official diagnosis in the third edition of the DSM largely in response to the large numbers of Vietnam Veterans suffering from this syndrome. Everything old is new again.

What are some treatments for PTSD?

Treatments for PTSD include medications and psychotherapy. The only two medications with Food and Drug Administration approval for PTSD are sertraline (brand name: Zoloft®) and paroxetine (brand name Paxil®), although other medications have been shown to be helpful for some PTSD sufferers. As for psychotherapy, clinical trials strongly support the use of various types of trauma-focused cognitive-behavioral therapy (CBT). Of the trauma-focused CBTs, prolonged exposure (PE) and cognitive processing therapy (CPT) have been used throughout the Department of Veterans Affairs (VA) hospital system. These and other treatments will be described in detail later in this book.

Are human beings resilient?

It is important to remember that experiencing traumatic events is part of being human. We are animals, and we live in a dangerous world. Luckily, with our medical advances, we are more likely to survive a trauma than were our ancestors even a generation ago. It is also important to understand that most of us will turn out just fine after experiencing a traumatic event. We are resilient, but there is no resilience without adversity.

We want our children to experience some difficulty to learn how to cope in life. We don't want everything to come too easily to them or for our kids to think that we will fix all their problems. In any good novel, the heroes often suffer some trauma or other problem early on, only to triumph in the end, usually due to skills they develop following that trauma. To become competent adults, we need to develop these skills. But where is the line between what harms us or helps us grow? How do we know which traumatic events will build our character or cripple us? Is it true that what doesn't kill us makes us stronger? How do we change that trajectory in the aftermath? We will explore these questions in *PTSD: What Everyone Needs to Know*.

1

HOW DO PEOPLE REACT
TO TRAUMA?

Cynthia awoke in the middle of the night to a hand over her mouth, feeling something sharp against her neck, and a voice in the dark saying, "Don't scream or I'll cut you."

As we ask in the introduction to this book, where is the line between what harms us or helps us grow? How do we know which traumatic events will build our character or cripple us? How do we change that path following a trauma? In general, we will look at the characteristics of the traumatic event (what happened) and at the person (who it happened to), important factors that can help determine the reaction (whether the trauma will lead to harm or growth).

Based on many years of research, we now know that different events have different risk factors: For example:

- Car crashes are very common in the United States, but most people who survive car crashes will be just fine.
- Many people think of posttraumatic stress disorder (PTSD) as the "war Veterans' disease," but most war Veterans are discharged without PTSD and often come home with stories of heroism, comradery, and a sense of accomplishment and growth from their service.
- About one half of women who are raped develop PTSD by one month after the assault; the number is higher in men who are raped.

- When survivors receive caring social support after a traumatic event, this support helps them recover. On the other hand, if loved ones respond by blaming the survivor, with anger at the survivor, or with a sense that the survivor should "get over it," these survivors are at increased risk of developing PTSD.
- Some lucky people are just genetically predisposed to higher levels of resilience and are more likely to recover following a traumatic event.

In this chapter we explore risk and resilience following trauma.

What are some common reactions to trauma?

Shortly after a traumatic experience (such as a sexual assault, car accident, combat exposure, or natural disaster), it is normal for survivors to experience many of the symptoms that we might later say are PTSD. However, for the first several weeks to months, these symptoms can actually be a normal part of the recovery process for many people, as we discuss next.

Fear and anxiety

During a traumatic event, feelings of fear and anxiety are normal. After the trauma, things that remind you of the trauma can trigger anxiety and the feeling of danger. Such reminders may be certain places, times of day, specific smells, or any situation that reminds you of the trauma.

Re-experiencing

In the weeks following a trauma, it is common and normal to have images or repeated thoughts about the traumatic event pop into your head. For some people, this can be so repetitive or intense that it interferes with their day-to-day functioning for a few days or weeks. But if these survivors continue to engage with life and approach the experience on their own terms, the re-experiencing events tend to get less frequent and less intense with time.

Avoidance

On the other hand, some people may begin to avoid thinking about the memory or avoid things that remind them of the trauma. For example, it is not uncommon for people who have been involved in a serious car crash to feel hesitant before they get behind the wheel again. If this avoidance is mild or only lasts for a short time, then the trauma survivor will likely still recover on their own. If, however, a survivor begins to truly withdraw from life and the avoidance gets worse, it may be helpful to seek professional help to look at the avoidance and to learn about the best ways to reduce the chances of long term mental health issues.

Sleep problems

In addition to fear, anxiety, re-experiencing, and avoiding following a trauma, it is common for survivors to have problems sleeping. Sometimes this is due to not wanting to have nightmares about the trauma or fear of being vulnerable when asleep, and other times the problems happen all on their own. As with the other reactions, trouble with being able to sleep usually gets better. If it does not improve or if the survivor wants help to sleep, often primary care providers can offer help—either with medication or psychotherapy.

Anger

Many survivors develop upsetting emotions following a traumatic event, including anger. These negative emotions may be understandable especially if someone harmed the survivor intentionally or if the traumatic event occurred due to someone's dangerous or neglectful actions. However, such negative emotions may be exaggerated and out of proportion—for example, the Veteran blaming command for decisions made and reacting with rage that doesn't lessen. These emotions may be helpful or unhelpful for the person, but if such feelings are not looked at, they can create unhelpful thoughts for the survivor about herself and the world. We don't want the trauma survivor to get stuck in anger. These emotions are normal and tend to get better with time if the survivor continues to talk about her feelings and, in her own way, to talk with supportive others (such as a family member, close friend, or therapist) about the trauma and what it means to her. If you are a survivor or know someone who is, and you would like help with any reactions that may develop following a traumatic experience, we encourage you to seek that help. Also know that for most survivors, these reactions will get better with time if they do not avoid thinking about the memory or reminders of the event.

Guilt and shame

Feelings of guilt and shame are very common following a traumatic event. Sometimes people blame themselves for things they did or didn't do to survive or to help others survive.

Grief and depression

Grief and depression are also common following a trauma. These feelings can include hopelessness and despair. A trauma survivor might cry more often or not at all. He might lose interest in the people and activities he used to enjoy. He may feel that plans he made for the future no longer matter or that life isn't worth living. He might also grieve for the life that he once had or planned to have.

View of the world and oneself

Trauma can change our view of the world and our self-image in a negative way. The trauma survivor may tell herself, "If I hadn't been weak or had not done that, this wouldn't have happened to me." She might feel more negative about herself after the trauma.

It is also common to see others more negatively and feel that people can't be trusted. For example, if a survivor used to think that the world was relatively predictable and safe, trauma can change that view. It can convince her that the world is dangerous and others aren't to be trusted.

Relationships and emotional numbing

If the trauma survivor feels like he can't trust anyone and if it is hard to feel close to people, intimacy—both emotional and physical—may also become very difficult. This change can impact sexual relationships. Some people find it difficult to want to have sex or even be interested in it following a traumatic event. This can be caused by a change in trust and also because of the emotional numbing. If a trauma survivor is trying to not feel anything negative, this can also interfere with his ability to feel anything positive. If you kink the hose to prevent cold water from flowing, it also prevents the warm water from flowing.

Alcohol and drug use

Another way of numbing or trying to change the way you feel is through the use of alcohol or drugs. While there is nothing wrong with responsible drinking, if the trauma survivor is using it to change how she thinks or feels about the trauma, this can become a problem. While increased drinking or drug use can offer a temporary fix, this substance use often slows down recovery and causes problems of its own.

What are some risk factors for longer term problems following trauma?

Early identification of risk factors could help healthcare providers prevent or limit symptoms before a problem develops for a trauma survivor. This "risk assessment" right after the trauma has occurred—combined with treatment for those at risk—could benefit many survivors who might otherwise develop long-term problems. It is estimated that 70 percent of us will experience a potentially traumatizing event in our lives, and 6 to 8 percent of that group go on to develop PTSD. In the following discussion, we explore reactions and risk factors for issues following a traumatic experience.

Can you give some examples?

For the rest of this book, we will follow Cynthia (who experienced sexual assault) and Thomas (who experienced combat in the Iraq War) to provide illustrations of how the process of trauma exposure can impact survivors who go on to develop PTSD. We will also discuss Lucia, who experienced a motor vehicle crash and participated in an early intervention study in the emergency room where she was brought and who did not go on to develop long-term PTSD. These stories and other briefer accounts (also referred to as "cases"), were created from our combined clinical experience of over 50 years working with trauma survivors and people with PTSD. Lucia, Thomas, Cynthia, and the others are not real people, but their stories include elements from different people we have worked with. These case examples contain disturbing material, and we want to warn you that some of the details may be upsetting to read.

Cynthia

Cynthia awoke in the middle of the night to a hand over her mouth, feeling something sharp against her neck, and a voice in the dark saying, "Don't scream or I'll cut you." She was paralyzed with fear. She smelled alcohol and stale sweat on her attacker. He forced her to perform fellatio and raped her vaginally and made her say that she liked it. He threatened that if she called the police, he would come back and kill her, and he knew where she lived.

Cynthia was a junior in college at the time of the assault. She had been out dancing that night with friends and always wondered if her rapist was someone from the club who followed her back home. For months following the assault, Cynthia was too scared to sleep at night. She watched TV until all hours, left all the lights on, and would finally fall asleep exhausted about 6 am. She missed more classes than she attended and couldn't concentrate on her assignments or complete her homework. She hated the touch of her boyfriend's hands on her body and never told him what had happened. After several weeks of her avoiding his calls and any contact, they broke up. She stopped going out with friends and took incompletes in all of her classes that semester. She finally went to the college counseling center, which referred her for assessment and then treatment for PTSD.

Thomas

Thomas was on his first deployment to Iraq and was driving back to base when he ran over an improvised explosive device (IED) that blew up his Humvee. The blast disoriented him and knocked out his hearing for at least a few minutes, with loud ringing for hours more. His vehicle filled with smoke, and he smelled burning flesh. By the time he could respond, he understood that his vehicle was on fire, and he worked to open his door and get out. Thomas fell to the ground as he exited his vehicle realizing that his right leg was badly injured and bleeding.

His thoughts turned immediately to the three other men in the vehicle, and he went to check on them. He opened the back door and helped pull out Washington who had been sitting right behind him. Washington was conscious but stunned and appeared to be injured but possibly not seriously. The two of them moved as fast as they could to the other side of the vehicle to try to extract their two comrades from the front and back seats. The vehicle was in flames at this point. Soldiers from the Humvee behind theirs were already trying to extract the other two soldiers from Thomas's vehicle. Sanchez, in the backseat, was badly injured and burned, but he survived; Ferrara, in the front seat, did not.

Thomas tried to help the medic attending to Ferrara, but the medic told Thomas to lie down as he was injured. Thomas was medevacked to the hospital, and when stable, he was flown back to the United States for continued care. His leg was too badly injured to return to Iraq, and he was medically discharged from the army.

With rehabilitation, Thomas was able to walk again and tried to pick his life back up where he had left it when he was deployed. But he found that he was emotionally distant from his wife, Christine, and their two young children. He was angry, drinking too much, and having problems sleeping. Christine finally told him that he had to get treatment, and he went to his local Veterans Affairs (VA) hospital where he was assessed and diagnosed with PTSD.

Lucia

Lucia, a 26-year-old, married, Hispanic woman was brought to the emergency room by ambulance following a motor vehicle crash in which she was the driver of a car that was totaled by a semitruck. She reported a brief loss of consciousness immediately after her car was struck and numbing and disbelief upon consciousness and resulting overall body pain and bruising.

Lucia is an elementary school teacher commuting from her home to the school where she teaches first grade in a suburb about 20 miles from her apartment. It generally takes her about an hour to drive in the mornings and about 30 minutes to return home in the afternoons as traffic isn't as bad then. As she was driving to school on a rainy morning, traffic was even worse than usual due to the bad weather. She was listening to the news on the radio as she was planning her day. Out of nowhere, she heard the loudest crash she had ever heard while feeling a huge jolting impact. Before she understood what was happening, she and her car were spinning around. She felt her body straining against the seat belt and being jerked around, like she was on a ride at the fair. Seeming like it was happening in slow motion, Lucia was now facing oncoming traffic and was terrified as she realized that a huge semitruck was barreling toward her blowing his horn. At this point she felt another huge impact that jerked her all around and against her seat belt and the door and the steering wheel. The last thing she remembers is thinking that this is it, this is when she is going to die.

The next thing she knew, she was in an ambulance. She could hear the siren and feel the ambulance as it was racing around cars. Lucia was disoriented and asked the emergency medical technician (EMT) who was working on her what happened. As she is asking, she is realizing that she is in pain and that she can't move her head. She has an IV in her arm and the EMT is calling out Lucia's vitals to the driver. She is starting to feel panicky and starts crying, but the EMT responds in a calm, reassuring tone, telling her that she is in an ambulance heading to the hospital; she was in a motor vehicle crash and was injured but she should be fine. Since Lucia hit her head during impact, she is being treated as if she might have spinal cord injuries, so she has sandbags beside her head and she is strapped to a spine board, and this is why she can't move her head. They want it stabilized until they can tell if she has any spinal injuries. Lucia can feel the fear rising, worrying what will happen to her if she has spinal injuries. What if she is paralyzed? What if she can't walk or take care of herself? She had thought she was going to die and felt lucky when she opened her eyes in the ambulance and realized she wasn't dead, but she is now terrified that she could be seriously injured.

The EMT sees that Lucia is upset and tries to reassure her. She asks Lucia if she is in pain and gives her IV pain medication. Lucia feels herself get a little sleepy immediately and calms down as she feels drowsy. The EMT tells Lucia that she thinks she will be OK, but she should try not to move until they can check her out at the hospital. She repeats to Lucia that they are treating her as if she could have spinal injuries just as a precaution.

When they arrive at the hospital emergency room, Lucia feels bounced around as her gurney is pulled out of the ambulance and she is wheeled into the ER. All she can see is straight above her since her head is sandbagged and strapped to the board. She sees the ceiling lights, feels the difference in the air temperature as they whisk her through different areas, smells hospital odors, hears voices and noises, but can only see faces if they lean over her face very deliberately. It's a different limited perspective, and it is very disorienting not being able to see or take in anything around her, only what's straight above her.

She is suddenly worried about her purse and cell phone and wants to call her family to let them know what happened. She wants to call the school, too, to let them know she's not coming in today. She can't see and doesn't know who is pushing her, so she just blurts out where is her phone? Where is her purse? She needs to make calls. The nurse pushing her responds that her purse is on the gurney with her, and they will help her make calls in a few minutes as soon as she gets back from X-ray.

That is the first she has heard that she is heading to be X-rayed. Lucia and her gurney are "parked" outside of X-ray for some time waiting her turn. She hears someone say it's a busy morning due to the rain during rush hour. When it is her turn, they ask her several questions about what happened, her injuries, and if she might be pregnant. She starts crying again because she and her husband have been trying to get pregnant, but it hasn't happened yet, and now she worries if it ever will or if she would even be able to care for a baby if she is paralyzed. They lay a heavy lead apron over her to protect her reproductive organs from the radiation and move her body around to get different angles of X-rays and then put the sandbags back beside her head and strap her head back to the spine board while they await the results.

As it is such a busy day in the ER, all the patient rooms are filled, so Lucia is waiting in the hall for about 2 hours until a room opens up. She ends up spending almost the entire day in the ER. Her husband, Nick, was called and arrives within an hour. She feels better with Nick there, holding her hand. He leans over her face so she can see him and is very sweet and supportive. During this time, her doctor and nurse let her know that the X-ray does not show any spinal damage so they remove the sandbags, strap, and spine board. Lucia is much more comfortable and cries with relief. However, fears of serious damage linger. They are keeping her to assess for other injuries, including if she has a concussion (also known as mild traumatic brain injury or TBI) since she lost consciousness after hitting her head during the crash.

Once Lucia is in her own room, a policewoman comes in to take her report. In recounting what happened and piecing it together with

*what witnesses reported, Lucia was driving in the outside lane (i.e.,
the slow lane all the way on the right) of a four-lane fast-moving
interstate highway. A semitruck changed lanes into Lucia's lane
but wasn't far enough behind her and clipped the driver side rear
bumper, sending her rear spinning out and leaving her facing oncoming traffic as the semi was right behind her and moving too fast to
stop. Apparently the truck driver did slam on his brakes but still hit
Lucia's car head on. This deployed her airbags, which probably saved
her life, but Lucia was jerked all around and hit her head on the driver
window of her door which apparently knocked her out. Luckily, she
was wearing her seatbelt.*

*Witnesses called 911, and the ambulance arrived within min-
utes. They treated her as if she could have spinal injuries so removed her very carefully. Police arrived and gave the truck driver
a ticket. His semi rig was not severely damaged, and he resumed
his driving.*

Who is likely to get PTSD and who will be OK?

As we mentioned earlier in this chapter, trauma is a common
life experience, and despite this, most people do not develop
PTSD. So why do some trauma survivors develop PTSD and
others do not? Years of research have looked at this question,
and while progress has been made and continues with every
new study, there are still many questions that remain unan-
swered. However, the resiliency of the human spirit is clear.
People have survived and some even thrive after horrific
experiences. Think of how many people continued leading
productive lives even after surviving the atrocities of the
Holocaust. What is also apparent is that two people can experience the same trauma and have completely different responses, with one person moving on without mental health
consequences and the other becoming debilitated due to
mental health issues. Researchers continue to work to understand why this is the case in an effort to prevent the negative
mental health impact of trauma.

If someone thinks that their life is in danger or that they might be seriously injured, they are more likely to develop PTSD than if they don't feel in danger. For example, if Alex and Jake are walking down the street together and get held up, they might have different reactions. Alex may feel sure that the mugger just wants their money and will then leave them alone. Jake may think that the attacker is crazy on crack and might kill them. Even though people may think that Alex and Jake had been through the same event, in some ways this is not true: in Alex's event, his life was not in danger, and in Jake's event, it was. In this scenario, Jake would be more likely to end up with PTSD than Alex. It's always important to ask the trauma survivor what they were scared would happen.

What are common risk factors for trauma-related problems?

As mentioned several times before, some people develop PTSD following a traumatic event, while others do not. Research on the risk for enduring mental health issues (like PTSD) following trauma shows several factors that might increase a person's chances for mental health problems.

Negative social support

If you experience a trauma and the people in your life reach out to help, that greatly lessens your risk of developing mental health problems over time. This certainly does not mean that you wouldn't be upset right after the event, but it does mean that over time things would get easier. You can imagine that if the people in your family and community provide physical support (food or a place to stay) and emotional support (a kind ear to listen to what happened or someone to sit with you in the hospital), you would more likely be able to work through the trauma on your own terms and come out of the experience on the other side (everything else being equal, which it often is not). But if you felt that you could not rely on those around you or if you reached out for help and got angry responses or responses that blame you for your situation, you would be more at risk for lasting problems.

Sometimes a survivor feels that the support coming her way is negative, even when people around her do not mean it that way. This is because social support can actually feed an unhelpful pattern in PTSD where trauma survivors isolate themselves out of avoidance, or they may snap at people in anger, and the people around them react by "giving them space." The intention of the loved ones may be to let these survivors heal and have time, but trauma survivors who are having trouble often interpret this behavior as rejection, which feeds their isolation and anger even more.

In the case of Thomas, his commanding officer screamed in his face for hitting the IED, blaming Thomas in the debriefing following the incident. While his fellow soldiers came to his support at the time, the negative impact of his commanding officer's words left a deep wound that was made worse since Thomas already blamed himself since he had been driving. He never shared anything about the incident with anyone else after the debriefing. His avoidance meant he was not able to get any positive social support from his unit or his family after he returned. When he got home, Christine would criticize his drinking, and this further fueled his self-blame and increased his sense of isolation. Christine was intending to help by pointing out how his drinking was impacting the family, but Thomas felt she did not understand his situation and was not supporting him.

Other risks for developing mental health concerns following a trauma

Some things about the trauma itself can increase the chance for developing mental health issues. These include interpersonal trauma (another person, rather than, say, a natural disaster, causing the trauma), more frequent or physically injurious trauma, and trauma that occurs at a younger age.

In the case of Cynthia, the rape experience was a violation of her personal safety that undermined her sense of the world as a safe place. It was an interpersonal trauma where someone had acted toward her in a way to intentionally hurt and demean her. She began to see men as only out to have sex and saw herself as a vulnerable person who was weak and unable to prevent men from hurting her. Cynthia suffered physical injuries from the rape and suffered with pain for months until she started her PTSD treatment and received medical care for her injuries. The rape, physical injuries, violation of her safety in her own apartment, and interpersonal trauma placed Cynthia at increased risk of developing mental health issues over time.

People who experienced abuse or neglect in childhood have an increased risk of mental health problems following trauma. When childhood abuse survivors later experience trauma as adults, they may take that later trauma as further evidence that they are bad or unable to handle difficult situations and that the world is dangerous. When this happens, the risk is greatly increased for mental health issues to continue over time.

For instance, Thomas grew up in a chaotic household due to his father Michael's violence and drug use and his mother Mary's death when Thomas was just 7 years old. He reported that his father would often disappear for days and when he returned, he would berate and physically abuse Thomas. This situation continued until Thomas was removed from the home by his aunt Renee at age 9. While Thomas acted out as a child, his aggressive behavior stopped about 2 years after moving in with his aunt. Her firm and constant loving attention helped him learn new ways to interact with the world and provided a safe environment. Thomas's history of abuse and neglect placed him at a higher risk of mental health issues when he was exposed to a trauma in adulthood.

Research suggests that some people may be genetically or biologically predisposed to a higher risk for PTSD after exposure to a potentially traumatic event. Most of these studies have shown the increased risk occurs for people who experienced childhood abuse or neglect. Researchers believe that such exposure during childhood may lead to actual biological changes relating to fear, danger, attachment, and social support. *As previously discussed, Thomas had a history of abuse and neglect. While he was never genetically tested, he may have also had a biological or genetic risk factor.*

What is a helpful framework to better understand how we experience trauma?

One theory that has gathered strong support is called emotional processing theory. First developed by Edna Foa and Michael Kozak over the past 33 years, emotional processing theory has been expanded by many other PTSD researchers.

To understand the impact of trauma from the perspective of emotional processing theory, you must first understand how normal fear and other negative emotions work. In emotional processing theory, fear and other negative emotions are represented in normal memory as a "program" for escaping danger. The "fear structure" includes different kinds of information, including:

1. What it is we are afraid of, which is called the "feared stimuli" (e.g., a bear we encounter unexpectedly in the woods);
2. The fear responses (e.g., our heart rate increases); and
3. The meaning we associate with the stimuli (e.g., bears are dangerous) and the meaning we associate with our responses (e.g., fast heartbeat means we are afraid).

When a fear is realistic, we call it normal fear, and the fear structure contains information about how we can best respond to the real threat to protect ourselves, such as one of the three Fs: fight, freeze, or flee. So feeling afraid when we see a bear and acting to get away are appropriate responses and can be seen as normal and helpful reactions that keep us safe and help us survive. However, a fear (or other negative emotion) structure becomes a problem when:

1. The information in the structure does not accurately represent the world;
2. Unhelpful avoidance or strong emotional responses are triggered by harmless stimuli that are related to the trauma;
3. The fear responses and avoidance interfere with a person's daily life; and
4. Harmless stimuli and responses feel dangerous.

In the aftermath of a trauma, as we discussed in the beginning of this chapter, we know that most people have symptoms that would be called PTSD if they continue over time; these symptoms might include thinking about the trauma and having strong emotional reactions to things that remind the survivor of the trauma. Over time, however, if the survivor gets back to his daily life and back to doing the things that he needs to do to function, these reactions tend to lessen. This process is known as natural recovery, and for this process to occur, two things are necessary:

1. Survivors must allow themselves to think about the trauma and be around people, places, and situations that remind them of the trauma.
2. When survivors think about their trauma and approach/ engage with trauma-related situations, they have the opportunity to learn that *thinking* about the trauma is not dangerous and also that trauma-related situations, people, and places are not dangerous. Such survivors can learn that they can do what they need to do in life and they can handle negative emotions.

By getting back to their lives and approaching (rather than avoiding) trauma memories and reminders, survivors learn that they can tolerate these situations and that nothing bad happens. They also learn that their feelings of distress go down even while they are confronting what they have been avoiding. They learn that they don't go crazy or lose control. Through natural recovery and approaching, survivors can tell the difference between the traumatic event and other similar but nondangerous events. They can see the trauma as a specific event occurring in space and time and see that the world is not wholly dangerous, and they can handle bad things when they happen. In Chapters 3, 4 and 6 of this book, we list some helpful and effective websites and apps for trauma survivors, their loved ones, and others who are interested in learning more.

What is posttraumatic growth?

It's important to remember when discussing increased risk for mental health problems following trauma that all of these factors lead to only a small to moderate increase in risk for mental health issues. Most trauma survivors still eventually recover and do not suffer with mental health issues in the long term. In addition, some people report positive changes following trauma. This posttraumatic growth refers to a sense of positive change following exposure to traumatic experiences. While most of this chapter has focused on the risk of developing mental health issues following trauma and on common reactions to trauma, resilience is by far the more common outcome for trauma survivors. We continue to be surprised at the strength and fortitude of the human spirit to make it out of tough circumstances to survive and thrive. For many people, they experience a sense of accomplishment for making it out of a tough situation or for surviving the trauma. For others, they realize that before the trauma they did not know what was important to them, whereas after surviving, they have a real sense of how precious life can be and feel that their values are more in line with their lives as a result. Research on posttraumatic growth has suggested that many trauma survivors experience both mental health issues resulting from trauma and posttraumatic growth at the same time. *In the case of Thomas, this was clear: He was proud of his military service and friends, and he felt a sense of accomplishment for the many combat missions he had completed. At the same time, he felt he was to blame for the IED incident. Indeed, for Thomas, his sense of accomplishment is what drove him to go to the VA for treatment when urged by Christine. He thought the VA providers might be able to understand his situation.*

What about physical health or chronic pain following a traumatic event?

Very often traumatic events include a physical attack or injury that requires treatment and healing. Sometimes, these injuries take a while to heal or result in chronic pain. Some survivors have told us when they feel pain, it reminds them of the traumatic event, and this leads to more distress on top of the pain. If this is the case, receiving treatment for PTSD can help this distress triggered by the pain.

Research has shown that survivors of traumatic events can suffer from poor physical health following the trauma. There are several theories about why this might be happening, but all agree that if there is distress (PTSD, anxiety, depression, substance misuse, and so on) following a traumatic event, this distress should be treated, which may then help with physical health. Survivors of traumatic events should follow good health practices (even if they don't feel like it), such as seeing healthcare practitioners regularly, following their instructions, eating healthy, exercising, and not misusing substances or smoking cigarettes. Having poor health on top of distress about what happened just adds insult to injury (literally).

In some cultures, the distress is expressed in physical symptoms such as, "I have headaches," "I'm tired," or "attaque de nervios." In rural American contexts, the term "nerves" can be used to describe anxiety and possibly PTSD symptoms. We have learned to take "I'm tired" as a possible indication of depression and assess the survivor accordingly.

Is it possible to prevent the harmful effects of trauma?

YES! When we know someone is at risk for problems following trauma, we can work to increase their chances for natural recovery. Allowing ourselves to think about, write about, and talk about the traumatic experience is helpful to emotionally process the event. Not getting into the habit of avoiding thoughts or feelings or things related to the trauma is also helpful. In Chapter 2 of this volume, we discuss many resources available and what helps to prevent the development of PTSD, including the idea that providing (a) social support and (b) resources as people desire them are key.

How do thoughts, emotions, and behaviors relate to each other?

Most of the treatments that have been shown to help PTSD and that we discuss in Chapter 4 of this volume are cognitive behavioral treatments (CBT). The cognitive behavioral model (as illustrated in Figure 1.1) includes three parts: thoughts, behaviors, and emotions. These three elements work together to bring about the emotions, thoughts, and behaviors within any given situation. Each element influences the next element in

Figure 1.1. General cognitive behavioral model of emotion.

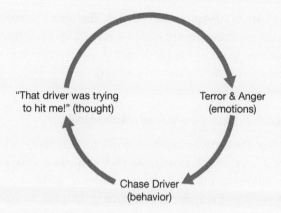

"That driver was trying
to hit me!" (thought)

Terror & Anger
(emotions)

Chase Driver
(behavior)

Figure 1.2. Driver in negative emotion cycle.

the process to lead to our thoughts and actions in a given situation. The model can begin at any element.

For example, let's consider a situation where a young man named Josh is cut off in traffic by a fast-moving vehicle. If the **thought** that Josh has in that situation is, "That driver was trying to hit me," then Josh is more likely to feel fear (**emotion**), anger (**emotion**), and defensiveness (**emotion**), and be extremely upset (**emotion**). As illustrated in Figure 1.2, Josh may react by speeding up to follow the other driver (**behavior**) and confronting him (**behavior**) or possibly by pulling off the road to rest and recover (**behavior**). If, instead, Josh's **thought** associated with being cut off is, "Good thing I saw that car coming and slowed down to let him in. I am a good driver," then he may feel pride/happiness (**emotion**) and may just continue on to work (**behavior**), as shown in Figure 1.3.

Each of these elements may shift significantly based on the one before and will influence the next element. In addition, we can start this cycle at any one of the three parts. In simple terms, our thoughts influence our emotions, and these influence our behavior.

Let's go back to our driver, Josh, who is feeling terrified. If he pulls off the road (**behavior**), he may have **thoughts** like, "I

Figure 1.3. Driver in return to baseline emotion cycle.

let people bully me. I am incompetent to do simple things like drive to work." This thought can lead to the **emotion** of sadness, and the cycle continues to deepen into a negative spiral. If, however, Josh **thinks**, "I will feel better in a minute. Anyone would be upset after almost getting hit," then the cycle does not increase negative **emotions**; the person will continue what they were doing, and it won't influence their **behavior**.

For most people, our life experience and thoughts about ourselves influence the likelihood of certain thoughts over others even given the same information. This is normal and makes sense since our brains are always trying to figure out patterns in the world to help us survive and thrive. However, sometimes these patterns may be inaccurate as a result of negative experiences that we do not want to have again. These unhelpful or dysfunctional thoughts are instances where our patterns of thinking don't really represent our current circumstances. They aren't based on the facts of the current situation and may influence us to act in ways that really don't help us. For many people, this bias or unhelpful thought pattern is something that they can notice and work to change on their own. For instance, if Maria's mother told Maria that she was selfish for not sharing enough with her brother, Maria may move into adulthood thinking that she is a selfish person. When other people respond to Maria differently as she does generous things, she may fall back into the pattern from childhood of viewing herself as selfish, or she may incorporate this new information and move to a new thought like, "I did not share with my brother as a child because I was immature, and now I have grown and learned how to be generous."

An example of this with trauma survivors occurs when child sexual abuse survivors think that all men or women are only out for sex, based on the survivor's experience with male or female perpetrators. These thoughts are often the target of PTSD treatments, and effective treatments work to improve trauma survivors' sense of their ability to handle negative thoughts and emotions and to better understand those situations in which they are safe from situations in which they may be at risk.

Does treatment affect the trauma memory?

Depending on the situation and desires of the trauma survivor, treatment can impact the memory of the traumatic event in various ways. Some of these are discussed next.

Will treatment erase the memory?

Many trauma survivors wonder whether they could just erase the trauma memory from their brains. They obviously wish it had never happened, and since we can't change that, the next best thing that survivors think is to erase the memory so they can act like it never happened.

For example, consider the case of Ann. After the rape she just wanted to never think about it again. She wanted to pretend it had never happened. She had not told anyone what had happened, and she did not know who assaulted her. For the first week after the rape, Ann went out dancing every night; she was drinking heavily and using other drugs to numb her feelings of terror when she had to go to the restroom (the rape occurred in the restroom of a club). After a week of very little sleep and heavy substance use, her body collapsed, and she slept the entire weekend. When she woke up Monday morning, she felt terrified and called in to work to say she would not be coming in that day. From that day forward until seeking treatment, Ann only went back and forth to work and home, and she never used a restroom with more than one stall in which the door couldn't be locked. When she arrived for treatment, she asked if there is any way to just take the memory out of her head.

While that is not possible, trauma-focused psychotherapies can help survivors reduce the intensity of emotions connected to the memory so that they can think through what it means about themselves and the world in a new way. Often this can result in the survivor noticing the things that they did to survive and feel good about these behaviors. Seeing their own competence in a time of horror, terror, or fear can go a long way toward helping trauma survivors feel able to handle the memory and interact with the world again. In addition, once the intensity of emotion is reduced, survivors are often able to reconsider some of the assumptions or conclusions they have made that are unhelpful or wrong.

For Ann, this involved reconsidering her thought that she was stupid for going to the club on her own that evening and that this meant she was just asking for someone to take advantage of her. She was able to see that this person did not target her, but was waiting to victimize whoever entered that restroom stall. She was able to recognize that it was OK for anyone to go to a club alone. Ann was in the wrong place at the wrong time, but not because she did anything wrong. She did not need to be ashamed of herself.

Instead of **erasing** the memory, trauma-focused therapies work with survivors to **change** the memory, to know what happened and honor the way that they survived while recognizing anything that they may want to change. This trauma is something that happened and we cannot change that, but we can change how we see ourselves and our reactions to the memory.

What about research that is trying to change how the memory is stored?

Some researchers are working on ways to change how the memory is stored following trauma by having survivors take certain medications right after the event. The idea for this line of research came from the desire of trauma survivors to erase trauma memories as well as research with rats and mice suggesting that fear learning can be effectively blocked with certain medications. To date, these efforts have not been much used in people because (a) the medications need to be taken within an hour or so after trauma exposure, (b) most of the drugs used in animals would be toxic to humans, (c) human trauma learning is very complex, and (d) we actually should remember when dangerous things happen to us so we can learn from them.

What about when survivors don't want to forget?

For other trauma survivors, they feel that changing how they think about the trauma or erasing the trauma feels like it would not honor the memory of others who endured the trauma with them or didn't survive. We will often hear this from Veterans who talk about their fellow Servicemembers who died or those who survived with them. For these trauma survivors, there is a piece of the memory that is positive and affirming of their job in the military and the work of others. They fear that if they stop being upset by the trauma, they might forget people about whom they care greatly—their brothers and sisters in arms. In these cases, therapists work with the survivor to explain that trauma-focused therapy does not remove the memory, it simply reduces the intensity of negative emotion and distress associated with it. We assure such survivors that they couldn't forget their comrades if they tried, and we are not asking them to forget. In this way, the survivor can have a greater sense of remembering that person and seeing the positives as well as the tough trauma that he (the survivor) endured. It helps when the trauma survivor gains the perspective that if the situation had been reversed, the survivor would want his friend to live a good life and not be haunted by what happened. Life is precious, and the friend would want the survivor to live it fully. His friend would want this for him.

What about survivors who feel the memory is taking over their lives?

Other trauma survivors feel that the trauma is something that has shaped who they are now. They do not necessarily want to lose that sense of themselves, and they just don't want the memory to take over when they think about it. For these survivors, the therapist can focus on how the processing of trauma memories allows the survivor to move through the memory in a new way. Once the distress associated with the memory is reduced, the survivor will have the chance to go back and consider all that happened at the time of the trauma, what she did and did not do, what factors may have contributed to making the decisions she made at the time, what context led to this happening, and so on. Through this processing of the memory, the survivor can figure out what she wants to take from the trauma as well as what she wants to change about how she sees or thinks about the trauma (what she wants to throw away). The survivor leaves with a more complete and full sense of the event, its context, and what that says about her as a person both at the time of the trauma and now. It is a balance of incorporating this event into her history and who she is as a person, yet not being defined by it.

What is good advice following a trauma?

We hear advice for how to take care of ourselves every time we fly: If the oxygen mask drops, place our mask on our face first before assisting others. People very often try to help others and place their own needs last. Especially following a traumatic event when others' needs are so great, some people may not be able to stop trying to help. We see this often following mass or natural disasters: Responders see such great need that they work double and triple and even quadruple shifts and then fall over exhausted. If we exhaust ourselves, we are no use to others. *It is always important and allowable to take care of ourselves.* We are not being selfish; we are being smart and responsible.

2

WHAT HELP IS AVAILABLE TO THOSE WHO HAVE EXPERIENCED TRAUMA?

A psychological concept known as Maslow's hierarchy of needs helps us understand how to help trauma survivors. *Basic human needs* include food, water, warmth, and rest. These basic needs are closely followed by our *safety needs* to make sure we are safe and secure. In Maslow's system, *psychological needs* follow once the basic and safety needs are met. Psychological needs include belongingness and love, which are met by intimate relationships and friends, followed by esteem, which is met by feelings of prestige and accomplishment. Only once our basic, safety, and psychological needs are met can we even consider achieving the pinnacle of Maslow's hierarchy of needs: *self-fulfillment needs*. This is what Maslow called self-actualization or achieving one's full potential in life.

Making sure the trauma survivor is physically taken care of and has access to necessary resources is the first way to help. This includes providing food, water, warmth, shelter, and medical care. The next levels are where social support plays an important role. People often tend to blame themselves, even for events not completely under their control, and survivors even more so, so it is very important that survivors feel there are people in their corner who are not blaming them for what happened. Giving trauma survivors an opportunity to emotionally process the event is one of the most important things that we can do to help. Giving them a space to talk about it, talk about it, talk about it—as much as is necessary to emotionally process the trauma—is equally as important. In addition, survivors have some specific needs depending on the type of trauma experienced. In this chapter, we expand on what the trauma survivor needs by looking at survivors of rape, interpersonal violence, child abuse, natural disasters, and burns, as well as looking at the people who step into harm's way to protect the rest of us—first responders and combat Veterans.

What do rape survivors need immediately after the assault?

Call the police

Although many rape survivors are hesitant to tell anyone, rape is a crime and should be reported to the police. The police can gather information and evidence to increase the chances that the perpetrator will be caught and prosecuted. If it was an acquaintance rape, the survivor may be even more hesitant to contact law enforcement, but it is still important to call the police. Even if the survivor does not want to press charges, calling the police and gathering the evidence keeps the options open. We have seen many rape survivors who later changed their minds about prosecuting, and then it was more difficult to move ahead as there was no physical evidence gathered or police report filed. If the assault occurred on a college campus, the campus authorities and campus police should be informed as well. In addition to legal charges, if the assailant was a student, there may be university actions against him or her, including expulsion.

Staying with the rape survivor until the police or ambulance arrives will help tremendously. She or he will likely be shocked, upset, physically in pain, and possibly almost feeling that this is unreal. It is a good idea to ask her permission before you touch her as she is likely to be sensitive to being touched. Many rape survivors cannot wait to wash the smell of their attacker off their bodies and many feel dirty, so it is common for them to have a strong urge to wash themselves. Urge her not to shower or clean up as the police will need to gather evidence. She should not brush her teeth. If there could possibly be any evidence in her mouth, have her spit it into a plastic sandwich bag, seal it, and give it to the police when they arrive. She should not even drink anything if there is a chance that there is evidence in her mouth, as drinking could wash it away. Most first responders are trained to be compassionate, but old attitudes can still prevail, and sometimes the police can come across as blaming the victim. If this happens, it is important for the survivor to have someone to counter that, assuring her in front of the police that it wasn't her fault.

Go to the emergency room

As soon as the rape survivor is out of immediate danger, she or he should get to the emergency room (ER). Taking the survivor to the ER or calling the police or ambulance may be necessary. At the ER, the doctors will perform a rape exam that includes gathering evidence for a rape kit. These procedures are very difficult for the survivor to experience, and she may feel traumatized all over again. The rape exam includes an internal exam (with the doctor often dictating the results out loud), examination with a black light to look for semen, and gathering semen samples if the perpetrator was male. That means a vaginal, anal, and oral exam. The doctor will comb through the survivor's pubic hair to extract evidence that may include the perpetrator's pubic hair. The ER staff will photograph the survivor and her injuries, which will usually include photographing genitals and breasts. Her clothes will be retained as evidence and she will go home in strange clothes. If she happened to be wearing her favorite sweater that night, or he was wearing his most comfortable jeans when attacked, they're gone. This can all feel very dehumanizing to the survivor, especially given the fact that she has just been through a terrifying sexual assault.

Many ERs have SANE nurses. Sexual assault nurse examiners (SANE) are registered nurses who have completed specialized education and clinical preparation in the medical forensic care of the patient who has experienced sexual assault or abuse. Some ERs have special areas for rape survivors that are a little more private with specially trained staff such as SANE nurses.

Unfortunately, the survivor can expect to be at the ER for hours. If there are physical injuries requiring X-rays, scans, or stitches, it can be even longer. For some survivors, the time in the ER almost feels like an extension of the assault. However, it is necessary to have her wounds cared for and to gather evidence and document the assault. A friendly face of a supportive friend or family member can make a big difference.

What about blaming the victim?

The most important thing for a trauma survivor to hear is that it wasn't his or her fault. In some rape situations—such as when the assailant is an acquaintance or when the survivor is a prostitute, sex worker, or stripper—survivors hear callous comments by first responders and sometimes by their coworkers or acquaintances. Sex workers agree to have sex with clients in exchange for money. But as we discussed in the introduction to this book, rape is a crime of aggression using sex as the weapon. When someone does not agree to sex, it is rape. Just because someone may have agreed to activities with the perpetrator up to the rape doesn't mean he or she agreed to the rape. In acquaintance rape, the survivor may willingly participate in kissing, touching, and other sexual activities, but if she doesn't agree to sex, it is rape. Even if someone initially agreed to sex, if she changes her mind and the other person continues to have sex with her, it is rape. Just because someone is dressed sexy, it does not give another person permission to have sex with her without her agreement. She is not "asking for it"; she is merely dressing in a way that makes her feel attractive. There was an ad campaign recently defending survivors: "It's an outfit, not an invitation."

Even if the survivor made mistakes or had errors of judgement, nothing justifies someone hurting someone else or taking what is not offered. Sometimes we only consider it an error in judgment afterward, knowing how things turned out. It is important to remember that we only have access to the information in the moment. In our society, the only time someone has the right to hurt you is if the act is in self-defense and he or she is protecting himself or herself. That is not the case with rape. We make errors in judgment every day, from missing the trash can to crossing the line when we're driving, and hopefully no one gets hurt. Even if a survivor made an error in judgment and made decisions that left her vulnerable, such as getting into someone's car, drinking too much, or getting too intoxicated with drugs, this does *not* justify rape. You can agree to share your sandwich, but if someone takes your half without your agreement, that is stealing. We are allowed to change our minds about having sex, even in the middle of having sex, and our wishes must be respected. If they are not, it is rape. It is important to relay this attitude to the survivor and correct anyone around her who is blaming. Survivors blame themselves enough; they don't need anyone else fueling these thoughts.

Cynthia's night at the ER

Cynthia

We described what happened to Cynthia in Chapter 1 of this book. Cynthia was terrified to call the police because the assailant had threatened her if she did, and he did know where she lived, but she was also terrified not to call the police. She did call 911, and they stayed on the phone with her until the police arrived, announcing that the police were at her front door, and they didn't hang up until she had let the police in. The officers who arrived were specially trained in handling rape cases and were very thorough and compassionate. After taking her report, gathering evidence, and taking photos around her apartment, they took her to the ER. This ER had a special area for patients who had been sexually assaulted, staffed by SANE nurses, so they were also very kind and professional. A social worker was called who explained the process to Cynthia and stayed by her side except during the physical exams.

Cynthia cried almost continuously from the time the police came and throughout her time in the hospital. She was shaking and felt very nervous, vulnerable, ashamed, and embarrassed. She felt terrible that she couldn't give a description of the assailant because it had been completely dark in her bedroom. She kept wondering if it was someone she knew or who she might have encountered at the club that night or if he followed her home. Both the police and the social worker assured her that she did nothing wrong; the assailant was a sexual predator and had targeted her. They encouraged her to call someone but she was embarrassed. She didn't want to tell her boyfriend for fear of what he would think, and they hadn't been together all that long. She finally decided to call her best friend Judy who was very supportive and offered to meet her at her apartment when she was going to leave the hospital. Judy spent the next few nights with Cynthia, kept her company, fed her, and helped her call the building owners to report what had happened and have the damage to her apartment repaired.

Judy wanted to be supportive in the way that Cynthia needed her to be, so she said just that, and asked Cynthia to please tell her plainly what she wanted her to do or not do. Judy asked Cynthia if she wanted to talk about it and was there to listen nonjudgmentally and compassionately when she did want to talk. Judy didn't press Cynthia when she didn't want to talk and distracted Cynthia when she wanted to be distracted. Judy was careful of her facial expression: She wanted to convey support and compassion, not pity or pain. If survivors feel that you cannot handle the details or that it will cause you too much pain, they will shut down, and Judy was sensitive to convey to Cynthia that she could handle anything that Cynthia wanted to share. She conveyed to Cynthia that she was so sorry this had happened to her, she was in no way to blame, and that she would help her get through this. It was hard for Cynthia to allow Judy to stay and to take care of her, but she was very glad she did.

What is interpersonal violence, and what do survivors need?

Interpersonal violence is when someone is hurt by someone with whom they are in a relationship. This has been referred to as "battered women" or "domestic violence" in the past, but all genders are vulnerable to interpersonal violence by their partners. In the United States, an estimated one in three women have been sexually assaulted, and one in four have been victims of intimate partner violence (IPV). It is a myth that a person cannot be raped by their husband or wife or partner. The consequences include increased risk for mental and physical health problems such as depression, anxiety, eating disorders, posttraumatic stress disorder (PTSD), addiction, injury, chronic pain, and disability. Although research usually focuses on women in their 20s and 30s, IPV and sexual assault also affect older women. It is important to understand that IPV crosses all boundaries—occurring in all genders, across all socioeconomic classes, in all countries, in all religious groups, and at all education levels.

IPV survivors need all of the resources we described for rape survivors *and* many of the resources we describe later in this chapter for disaster survivors. To stop the abuse, they may need to leave their home and spouse or partner. It is not uncommon that they have to run away, slipping out when they can so that their partner doesn't try to stop and possibly hurt them. Therefore, they may leave with nothing but the clothes on their backs, sometimes escaping without cell phones, money, or identification. If there are children involved and they need to protect and care for the children too, their needs multiply. Oftentimes going to a friend's or relative's home may not be safe if their partner would know to look for them there. Many cities have shelters, but these are typically short-term, overcrowded, underfunded, and difficult to manage with children.

Of course, many IPV survivors do not choose to leave their partners for various reasons, and in such situations, nonjudgmental social support is very important. It is easy to judge and think, "I wouldn't put up with that; I would leave," but no one knows how they themselves would respond until they are in that situation. IPV survivors are already afraid and ashamed; they don't need their friends and loved ones piling it on. They need their friends and loved ones to say, "Whatever you need, I am here for you" and "Tell me what I can do for you to help." They may need information on resources so that they can see it is possible to get out if they do decide to leave.

IPV survivors have different needs depending on their circumstances. They tend to be even more hesitant than rape survivors about calling the police, both for fear that their partner will retaliate and concerns that their partner will be arrested. These survivors may truly love their partner, believing when the abuser says that the violence won't happen again, and they don't want their partner to get in trouble. It is possible to hate and love someone simultaneously—humans are very complicated, and life is very complicated. The IPV survivor may be financially dependent on the abuser, and they may fear that he or she will not support them and the children if they leave. If the survivor is still living with the abuser, anything that can help ensure safety is welcome. Having someone to turn to for nonjudgmental compassionate social support, material support, and shelter is very helpful. Helping the survivor gather information on resources if she is hurt, if she were to leave, how to obtain a restraining order, and so on is also valuable.

Someone living in this type of abusive household has to be very careful about texts, emails, contacts, and voicemails, as the abuser may check her phone and computer. Typically the IPV survivor should not bring any material about domestic violence into the home as this may enrage the abuser. Therefore, a supportive friend or loved one may need to develop a code or secret hiding place for material or allow the survivor a space in her own home to store such materials or even a "getaway bag." The National Domestic Violence Hotline has a warning on their website: "Safety Alert: Computer use can be monitored and is impossible to completely clear. If you are afraid your internet usage might be monitored, call the National Domestic Violence Hotline at 1–800–799–7233 or TTY 1–800–787–3224."

If the IPV survivor suffers an injury, the scenario is similar to what we discuss above about calling the police and going to the emergency room. Even if the survivor does not want to press charges, it is important to get medical attention and to document her injuries in case she changes her mind in the future. Being there to support her and letting her know it is not her fault, that no one has the right to hurt her or her children, is of the utmost importance. It is not useful to say bad things about the abuser, since that may make the survivor feel even worse and may make her reluctant to say something again. Interpersonal trauma survivors very often experience tremendous shame and guilt and at some level wonder if it is their fault. Abusers typically tell survivors that it is their fault: "You made me do it." Although clearly false, this message often gets inside a survivor's head and contributes to her shame.

If a survivor makes the very difficult decision to leave her abusive partner, this can take various forms. For example, some survivors have to escape when they get the chance and have literally bolted out of the house naked, running for their lives. These are often the situations in which abuse has been ongoing and is escalating, and the survivor fears for her life. Very often, this is accurate. It is important to remember that the majority of women who are murdered are killed by someone who they know. The other end of the spectrum is when someone has been planning to leave and has been trying to line up resources and make plans in secrecy, for fear of being discovered.

What can you do if you suspect childhood abuse?

Adults can decide if they want to report their own abuse; however, knowledge of abuse or neglect of children must be reported. Anyone who encounters that child and suspects abuse should ask about it in a warm and caring manner and then report it to the authorities if warranted or if the situation requires further investigation. Childhood abuse may include physical abuse, verbal abuse, sexual abuse, witnessing violence against others, and/or neglect.

If you suspect a child is being abused or neglected, or if you are a child who is being maltreated, contact your local child protective services office or law enforcement agency so professionals can assess the situation. Many states have a toll-free number to call to report suspected child abuse or neglect. Most states have a Division of Family and Children Services with a 24/7 reporting line.

As difficult as it is for adults to understand mistreatment, it is nearly impossible for a child to understand, and children nearly always blame themselves or feel that they are at fault. It is very confusing for a child when the person who takes care of him is also the person who hurts him. Very often children develop unnaturally close bonds with their abusers and become overly attached to them. So just because it appears that a child loves someone, it doesn't mean that that person is not hurting him.

A child will need to be protected from ongoing abuse or neglect, and that very often may require removing him from the home. Studies have shown that having one constant stable loving person in a child's life can help mitigate awful experiences. Be that person! Children need to hear repeatedly that the abuse was not their fault and that they are loved and valued and did not deserve to be hurt. We know that children are resilient, but we also know when bad things happen to children, they very often grow up into different adults than they would have been without abuse or neglect. Unfortunately, if a child is removed from the home and enters the foster care system, it is a very difficult path. Most foster families are wonderful, nurturing, and caring, but there are some who enter into foster care for the wrong reasons, and unfortunately, abuse and neglect may continue. It is heartbreaking when this occurs, be-cause the child starts to feel that he is truly all alone, no one can be trusted, and there is no one who can help. These are the very sad individuals who often end up on the street, making money any way possible—often through hustling, drug dealing, or prostitution—where they are often at risk for further violence.

The child's physical safety must be guaranteed, and at-tending to their emotional needs is nearly as important. There are several effective treatment programs for abused and neglected children and several programs in which their nonoffending parent or caretaker can participate. We will talk more about children in Chapter 5 of this volume.

What about survivors of natural disasters?

We have seen devastating earthquakes, hurricanes, tornadoes, floods, and forest fires—just in the past year. Natural disasters cause extensive damage to large areas sometimes affecting millions of people at the same time. Remember Maslow's hier-archy of needs? Natural disaster survivors need safe and warm shelter, clothing, food and water, and to be out of harm's way. There are many service organizations such as the Red Cross that assist in disaster relief. Once a state of emergency is de-clared, resources such as the National Guard may also be de-ployed to help.

Adding to the difficulty in providing for the needs of nat-ural disaster survivors is the fact that usually many people are affected at the same time, and the resources for that com-munity have often been impacted, for example, with power outages, contaminated water supplies, roads closed, and infra-structure blown. Survivors with physical or emotional condi-tions prior to the natural disaster are even more at risk, as they may enter the disaster in a weakened state. Disaster survivors may have been forced to flee without their medications or de-vices for their mental or physical support. The chaos and con-fusion of a disaster zone is hard on anyone. Imagine adding to that situation with any vulnerability or sensitivity and the result can be "decompensation," in which the person may not be in touch with reality and seems to have lost all ability to cope. In a hospital or medical setting, "triage" refers to the sorting of patients according to the urgency of their need for care. In a disaster zone, there is also emotional first aid and triage of sorts. Survivors who are visibly shaken or distressed should be attended to first in an attempt to get them settled. If those with existing conditions, such as serious mental health concerns can be identified, that will help ensure their needs are met, including prescription medication and safe, secure environments.

It can feel devastating to the disaster survivor who may have lost loved ones and all their material goods. As we mention throughout, after material needs are met, social support will be very important.

Who are first responders, and what are their needs?

First responders include police, firefighters, emergency medical technicians (EMTs) on ambulances, and other field and disaster responders. They include both paid professionals and volunteers, and they all see bad stuff. They run *into* danger when the rest of us are running away to safety. They arrive at life's worst moments and are witnesses to violence, injury, evil, death, devastation, and despair while it is still unfolding. Although they are trained to encounter this destruction, like military service members and Veterans (discussed later), they are human. Unlike the military, they are often on their home turf, and if they do not know the victims personally, they could, and they know the street and the neighborhood. We have heard, for example, about the many acts of heroism surrounding the Camp Fire in Paradise, California, in the fall of 2018, where firefighters were battling the fires while their own homes burned to the ground.

It is important for first responders and disaster workers to care for themselves and each other. We have heard of first responders who don't go home after their shifts have ended; instead they work two, three, or four or even more shifts and then fall over exhausted. People often do this out of a desire to be helpful when they see so much that needs doing. However, it is important to take care of oneself. As we mentioned in Chapter 1 of this book, the best example is in the introduction on an airplane: "If the oxygen mask falls, put your mask on first before you assist others." The one good thing to arise since the September 11, 2001 terrorist attacks on the World Trade Centers and the Pentagon in the United States is a greater understanding of PTSD in first responders. Police chiefs and fire chiefs are generally now more aware of PTSD and encouraging their men and women to take care of themselves and seek treatment.

However, there is still stigma associated with having PTSD or showing any sign of "weakness," especially in these professions that pride themselves on their bravery, strength, and strength of character, as well as in the military. PTSD warning signs may include avoidance of work, social isolation, increase of drug and alcohol use, anger outbursts, and other potentially self-destructive behaviors. One thing that first responders need is an atmosphere that allows them to disclose if they are having problems and without professional repercussions. We often use a sports analogy of getting injured, needing rehab, and then getting back in the game. Exercise is an excellent way to manage stress, but not if it is used to hide feelings or avoid issues.

As with disaster survivors, first responders require their basic needs of shelter, safety, warmth, rest, food, and water met first. As with any trauma survivor, it is important to allow them time and space to emotionally process what happened to them. The best ways to emotionally process these types of events are to think about them and talk about them in a nonjudgmental atmosphere. Often this is not the stuff of dinner table conversations with one's families, so it is helpful if first responders work in a supportive environment where they can discuss these events and their reactions with others who have experienced similar events and reactions. If this is not available, they need to seek it out in other ways, such as with friends, family, religious organizations, or mental health professionals. To people who pride themselves on taking care of others, one of the hardest tasks may be to realize when they need assistance themselves and then being in that role rather than being the caretaker or knight in shining armor.

What do military service members and Veterans need?

Service members and Veterans' needs are similar to first responders' needs. They run into danger to protect the rest of us; live in a "macho" atmosphere of bravery, strength, and protection; and can be judged for showing anything that others might consider to be weak. Military service members require their basic needs of shelter, safety, warmth, rest, food, and water met first. They need to be able to count on their comrades and want their comrades to be able to count on them unconditionally. They will do anything to help their battle buddies and are trained to respond, overriding their fear responses. Things are changing, but the military after-action report, where they review what happened and what went wrong, was typically a blaming/shaming experience. If something went wrong, it was someone's fault.

Veterans, like other trauma survivors, tend to believe their *stories* of what happened rather than the *facts*.

Thomas, who we first met in Chapter 1 of this volume, believed that since he was driving the Humvee when it was hit by an improvised explosive device (IED) and his friend in the front seat died, this tragedy was his fault. We often encourage Veterans to tell their stories in detail and repeatedly, and if there is blame, to share the blame. If Veterans have the chance to talk about what happened in the immediate aftermath in a nonjudgmental manner and in enough detail, this often helps them to emotionally process the event in a way that does not continue to haunt them. When they avoid the trauma or are blamed and feel guilty, it is more likely to haunt them day and night.

We have heard wonderful stories about smart first sergeants or chaplains doing their "walkabouts" after an event and checking in with service members who were involved and affected. They know the members in their unit and are in a position to identify early on if someone seems to be having a hard time and allowing him to talk about it in a nonjudgmental manner.

Service members and Veterans are often hesitant to talk to civilian friends and family members about the details of these events that might be haunting them. This is true for several reasons. They are protecting their loved ones from the loss of innocence that they have experienced. It is hard enough for the service member to make sense of what happened, and they have the training and the context. They know it would be hard for a civilian to understand. They also want to protect their loved ones from pain, including the pain of worrying about them or even knowing they are in pain. They are likely avoiding, not wanting to think about or talk about what happened and possibly not understanding these consequences as PTSD. They often feel guilty and ashamed, even when there is no objective evidence that they did anything wrong and may have acted with bravery. They may feel that they will get over it with time. They may also believe that since no one can change what happened, there is no use in talking about it.

Can you provide an example of a military service member who experienced a traumatic event?

Thomas

We can use Thomas as an example of what military service members and Veterans need. Remember Thomas was medically evacuated after the Humvee he was driving was hit by an IED. When he returned to the states, he was hospitalized at Walter Reed hospital in Bethesda, Maryland, for surgery on his right leg and rehabilitation. His wife, Christine, and two children met him there and were able to stay in the Fisher housing for families of service members while they are hospitalized at Walter Reed. In the hospital, Thomas was hoping to have his leg repaired and be able to return to his unit in Afghanistan. When it became clear that this wouldn't be possible, he became depressed, angry, and withdrawn. His family didn't completely understand why Thomas wasn't happy to be back in the states and with them and out of danger. Thomas didn't even try to explain his sense of duty and obligation to his buddies and his desire to avenge his friend's death.

Back in his Midwestern town, Thomas received care at the local Veterans Affairs (VA) hospital. They screened him for PTSD and depression and diagnosed him with both. All VA hospitals offer evidence-based care (see Chapter 4 of this volume), but Thomas wasn't ready. His more immediate needs focused on trying to get his old job back and reintegrating with his family and community. Luckily, he had worked for a Veteran-friendly employer and had been a stellar employee before his deployment so he was able to get his old job back. He found the new faces and new procedures a bit upsetting, and he would often easily get frustrated.

Thomas tried to slip back into his old routine at home but found that things had changed there as well. The kids were growing up, and his wife Christine had had to figure out how to get everything done that Thomas used to do, so she seemed quite capable and independent, and he felt like his family didn't need him. He retreated to the garage to drink beer alone every evening, drinking enough to help him get to sleep at night. He often awoke with nightmares and one time actually fell out of the bed when he was trying to run away in a nightmare. Christine was concerned; she tried to talk to him and soothe him, but he withdrew from her.

As PTSD treatment providers, we hear similar stories from many Veterans. Many enlisted out of a sense of patriotism and duty. Many returned home disillusioned, angry, and withdrawn; feeling different from everyone else around them; and feeling that their innocence had been lost. It is very important that these Veterans learn how to become civilians again and adjust to their civilian life style. A meaningful job and meaningful relationships help this process. They also need to retrain their bodies and brains that they no longer need to "stay alert, stay alive." The majority of Veterans do make this readjustment successfully and never are seen for care. However, when problems such as PTSD create barriers to this readjustment, the PTSD must be addressed. We will talk more about treatment for PTSD in Chapter 4 of this volume.

What about burn survivors?

Burn survivors obviously require immediate medical attention, but they have other specific needs. Burns are very painful for a long period of time. The care of burns is very painful, requiring "debridement," which is the removal of damaged tissue or foreign objects. Depending on the extent of burn damage, there may be loss of function requiring rehabilitative therapy. Burns leave scars, and scars are very noticeable. In addition to the physical pain and disability, burn survivors are dealing with the emotional aftermath and living the rest of their lives scarred and possibly disfigured. Burn survivors are typically treated with pain medication, which has been shown to help decrease the development of PTSD. Therefore, burn survivors should be supported in all that they need to do to recover, including participating in physical therapy (usually including wound debridement) and taking medications to help control the pain without stigma of taking pain medication. The emotional support that burn survivors require is similar to that of other trauma survivors: They need a supportive, nonjudgmental ear, and they also need help for more specific concerns about scarring and disfigurement.

What are common needs of trauma survivors?

We have already discussed specific needs of survivors of different types of trauma, but there are also common needs that most trauma survivors have.

Social support

We can't emphasize enough the importance of social support because social support is one of the most important predictors of who goes on to develop PTSD and other lasting difficulties and who does not. In fact, a *lack* of social support is one of the best predictors of who *will* develop PTSD. The intentionally helpful acts of another person can't totally get rid of the effects of the trauma, but such kindnesses can help manage the negative effects. As discussed earlier, it is important to be physically present for the trauma survivor and emotionally available, supportive, and nonjudgmental. Having someone nearby who doesn't blame the survivor for what happened and clearly just wants to help is the most precious gift a trauma survivor can receive. The trauma survivor is likely grieving. If she has lost a loved one, the grieving may be obvious, but she may also be grieving the loss of her innocence, her sense of safety, and her former appearance, if she was injured or disfigured.

Material support

All trauma survivors require their basic needs of shelter, safety, warmth, rest, food, and water met first. With some events such as natural disasters and fires, the survivor has experienced great resource loss that may require moving. They may have nothing but the clothes on their backs. The Red Cross is one agency that is tremendously helpful in trying to provide resources for trauma survivors. The assistance for victims of crimes varies state by state, and many states help with reimbursement for some losses and expenses, such as medical expenses, as a result of crime.

Medical care and resource support

If there are injuries, the trauma survivor requires physical support such as medical attention, caring for physical wounds, and medication. If the injuries interfere with normal day-to-day functioning, the survivor may need material assistance in carrying out his daily activities until he is healed. If the injuries prevent him from working, he will also need financial support if the survivor doesn't have resources such as disability insurance or income protection.

What should you not *say to a trauma survivor?*

When a trauma survivor confides in a friend or family member, there are a few reactions that are not helpful. For example:

- When a survivor of a motor vehicle crash wakes up in the hospital, it is not helpful for worried family members to say, "Oh my G-d, you almost died."
- When a woman tells her partner that she was raped, it is not helpful for her lover to say they don't know how they can touch her again or ask what did she do or how did she let this happen.
- When a child confides that he has been sexually molested or abused, it is not helpful for the trusted adult to say that the child must have misinterpreted what the abuser was saying or doing, that the child must be mistaken.
- It is not helpful for the domestic abuse survivor to hear it must not be that bad since she hasn't left, or what bad judgment she has in men.

The old adage is true: If you can't say something nice, don't say anything at all. If you don't know anything else to say, you can always just say, "I'm sorry this happened to you."

What you should *never* say

> "You must be mistaken."
> "What did you do?"
> "It can't have happened that way."
> "You were wrong."
> "Why didn't you leave?"
> "Why didn't you tell someone?"
> "You're lucky to be alive."
> "Adults know best."
> "He's so nice—he couldn't have done that to you."
> "It was your fault."
> "I can't look at you the same way."
> "I can't touch you now."
> "You knew this would happen."
> "This is war—what did you expect?"
> "Did you kill anyone?"
> "It doesn't sound that bad."
> "It couldn't have been that bad or you would have left."
> "Why didn't you scream?"
> "Why didn't you run away?"
> "Why didn't you fight?"
> "Why did you let him do that to you?"
> "I wouldn't have let him do that to me."
> "You're a wimp."
> "You have to toughen up."
> "What are you so upset about?"
> "What does it matter? He was the enemy."
> "Get over it."

What to *always* say

> "I'm sorry this happened to you."
> "I'm sorry you were put in this position."

"I'm sorry you had to make that awful decision."
"I believe you."
"I want to help in any way I can."
"It wasn't your fault."
"I still love you."
"I am proud of you."
"This doesn't change how I feel about you."
"Anyone in that situation would have done what
    you did."
"I can't imagine being in that situation."
"Whatever you did, you did the right thing because you
    are here to tell about it."
"I want to help but you may have to let me know how."
"You are a good person; this doesn't change that."
"Even people who others see as nice can do bad things."
"You did what you had to do to survive."
"I'm glad you survived."
"This doesn't change what I think of you."

What do families of survivors need?

The saying about the military, "When one person serves, the whole family serves," is true of all trauma survivors. The entire family is affected. As painful as it is to experience a traumatic event, it is also extremely painful to witness a loved one experiencing a traumatic event and its aftermath. As parents, many of us would rather experience a painful event than have our children go through it. We want to protect our loved ones and nurture them. When they have experienced a horrific event and are in physical and emotional pain, we feel helpless. We feel anger that this happened to them. We often blame ourselves that we didn't protect them better.

Trauma changes survivors, and it may be hard to know how this changed person fits into the family. They may be more irritable and distant. They may have strong reactions to noises, movements, or smells that they didn't have before. They may cry more easily. They may drink more alcohol or use more drugs. They may be overprotective of other family members. Family members make up a system, and when one family member changes, it affects how everyone else interacts. People often feel like they need to "walk on eggshells" to avoid upsetting the trauma survivor.

When the trauma survivor is dealing with his own issues such as anger, guilt, and fear, he probably doesn't need to take on the responsibility that his family is experiencing similar reactions. It may make the survivor feel more guilt to have caused his family this pain. But family members do not need to deny the impact of the trauma either. It's a matter of degree and the tone of the message. It is fine to let the survivor know something like, "I hate that this happened to you. It hurts me to see you hurt. But we are strong, we will get through this, and I will help you in any way that I can."

The line in the sand for us is always functioning. If the family functioning is disrupted, there are specific services that might be helpful. There are a number of services for military families. Smart pediatricians on military bases always ask where the parent is in the deployment cycle (e.g., preparing to deploy, deployed, or returned from deployment) to have an idea of the impact on the child and the parent at home. Partners of rape survivors may require some coaching to know how best to discuss the assault and how to approach physical and intimate contact. If the trauma survivor has a lasting disability following the trauma, this obviously affects the family. If the family member of a survivor is experiencing disruptions in their functioning as well, they may need to seek therapy on their own. The very best medicine for a family member of a trauma survivor is seeing their loved one recover and grow stronger. Very often, their own recoveries track the same course.

How can you help yourself?

We think it is important to emotionally process a traumatic experience. We do not think it is helpful to "soldier on" and avoid thinking about it. We make analogies to the grief process: The only way to the other side of the pain is through it. Writing or talking about it to others has been shown to reduce many of the negative health effects and help with readjustment. But not just once—talk about it, talk about it, talk about it, until you don't need to talk about it anymore (or write about it repeatedly, in detail, including your emotional reactions). And no one can say just when that is. You have to wear it out until you have talked or written about it as much as you need to.

If you don't feel you have someone you can talk to about it, find someone. Or write it out repeatedly. Or call a hotline. Or find a support group. Or seek professional care. Or talk to your clergy. If there is no one within your support system you feel you can talk to, go outside your support system. The point is, it won't go away on its own. You have to process it, and talking about it repeatedly, trying to make sense of it, is one of the best ways to process what happened.

We conducted a study of people in the emergency room who had experienced a traumatic event just hours earlier. Our treatment was to have them talk about what had just happened, repeatedly, in the present tense, for about 45 minutes. We recorded that account for them to listen to at home. We asked them not to avoid safe situations just because they reminded them of the traumatic event. We taught them a brief breathing relaxation method to practice and reminded them to take care of themselves and be nice to themselves for the next few days. People who received this treatment had one half the rate of PTSD 3 months later as compared to people who didn't. Talking about it in a therapeutic manner helps!

Many survivors are hesitant to talk about the trauma with friends or family members or even with professionals. They don't want to burden them or cause them pain or they are embarrassed, fearful, or ashamed. Ask yourself this: Would you want to be there for a friend or loved one after they have experienced a painful event? Most of us would say yes. Then let them be there for you. It is a gift you give them to let them feel like they are being helpful to you.

Most of us feel good when someone trusts us enough to share something important with us. It is a sign that they trust us and feel close to us. It is true that some people may disappoint you, but it is also true that many won't. You might be surprised by how many people truly want to help. You won't know until you try. There is a good chance it will help you, make them feel good about trying to help you, and strengthen your relationship. Sometimes the closest relationships are ones forged during difficult times.

You can also help yourself by not avoiding realistically safe situations just because they remind you of the traumatic event. If you were involved in a motor vehicle crash, for example, you need to get back out there and drive again, making sure to drive that vehicle when it is drivable and that intersection or wherever the crash occurred. You need to put yourself in situations that are realistically safe but may make you uncomfortable and to stay in them long enough for your body and brain to realize that they do not pose the level of threat that it initially felt like. If you need to take along a friend at first, that's fine, but don't become dependent on having someone with you if you used to be able to do it alone.

It is important not to increase substance use. Research found that following the terrorist attacks on the World Trade Center on 9/11, residents of Manhattan increased the use of all substances—alcohol, drugs, and cigarettes. This seemed to follow the course of PTSD, so substance use increased as PTSD increased. However, the substance use didn't decrease even when the PTSD did. Substance use is often another way to avoid. It has been shown to interfere with emotionally processing a traumatic event. One rule of thumb to follow is if something traumatic happens, don't use alcohol or drugs (other than those prescribed) until you have emotionally processed the event and its impact.

How can you help others who have survived trauma?

Being a nonjudgmental person to talk to is the best gift you can give to a trauma survivor. Letting him know he is not to blame for what happened, you are there for him, he is strong and you are too, and you will help him get through this will be so important. If he needs help while he is recovering or getting to appointments, it is important to do so graciously. If you resent doing it, you might as well not do it. If the survivor is continuing to have problems, helping him look into resources and discussing options can be helpful if he is open to it. If he is not open to it, letting him know that you are there and ready to help when he is ready is useful.

How do PTSD sufferers handle the reactions of those who love them?

It is important for the trauma survivor to keep in mind that her loved ones experienced a traumatic event as well. Even though she might think, "It didn't happen to them," something *did* happen to them because their loved one was seriously injured or in danger of serious injury or death. This actually is included in the American Psychiatric Association's fifth edition of the *Diagnostic and Statistical Manual of Mental Disorders* (DSM-5) definition of the traumatic event, so they might be experiencing PTSD as well. The definition of the trauma in the DSM-5 includes, "Exposure to actual or threatened a) death, b) serious injury, c) sexual violation, . . . learning that the traumatic event(s) occurred to a close family member or close friend; cases of actual or threatened death must have been violent or accidental." Even if a partner or other family member or loved one does not have PTSD, it is hard to see someone you love at risk or having trouble. Many trauma survivors with

PTSD have trouble feeling close or being close to people. For family and friends, this can feel like a loss or rejection, and this can be tough on the relationship.

In one of our books for professionals about PTSD following rape, a colleague whose daughter was raped when she was a teenager offered to write the opening chapter from the father's perspective. He describes his emotions that include anger, sadness, grief, concern, and worry. He felt guilty that he didn't protect his daughter. He felt terrible that she didn't disclose the rape to him when it occurred, especially since he was a psychologist and others told him their problems, but his daughter didn't feel like she could. It was hard to control the rage— he felt that he wanted to kill the man who did this to his daughter. He wondered if she could get over this and worried for her and her future. He was so angry, and for a while, that seemed to invade everything. He had to learn to control his anger around his daughter. He described that his recovery mirrored his daughter's: while she continued to suffer, he continued to suffer. When she started to recover, he started to recover.

Here is another example.

Another young man we treated, Jacoby, was injured in a terrorist attack while traveling on a mission trip to a small country that frequently had attacks by rebel fighters. Several people were killed in the bombing and the shooting that followed. He heard chaos and raced with others into a back room and barricaded the door. When they were discovered, he survived by hiding under dead bodies. He lost his cell phone and shoes in the chaos and hid under the bodies for over 5 hours while the rebels patrolled and continued to shoot people. When Jacoby was able to escape the building, he wandered the unfamiliar streets alone from hiding place to hiding place, not knowing who he could trust to help him or if he would encounter the killers or other rebels. He felt that he clearly looked like he was from the United States and would be killed if spotted by the rebels. He hid— cold, hungry, alone, and shoeless—behind a pile of rotting garbage for several hours until daybreak when he stopped hearing gunfire. When Jacoby was discovered, it was by the police who helped him get to safety.

Jacoby's parents knew he was there and heard that there was a rebel attack but had no word from him. They were up all night trying to get word and sick with worry and praying. They didn't know if their son was alive or dead or lying in the street bleeding to death and needing help. Obviously, they felt that their prayers had been answered when they received word that he was OK.

Jacoby stayed with his parents for a few weeks when he returned to the United States and sought treatment during that time. Besides his PTSD from the attack, he expressed anger at his parents. He felt like they gave him the third degree whenever he went out and questioned his decisions. They wanted him to check in with them constantly when he went out or even when he was home and they were at work. He felt like they were treating him like a child. He exploded at them when he overheard his mother talking with one of her friends about the attack. Jacoby said, "It wasn't hers to tell."

I explained to Jacoby that his mother did have a story to tell and that she needed to tell, although hers was a different story. It is true she and her husband hadn't experienced the bombing, gunfire, hiding under dead bodies, and hiding behind rotting trash, but they had experienced knowing that their son was possibly in an attack on the other side of the world and they didn't hear from him for almost 12 hours. During that time, they imagined the worst and didn't know if Jacoby was dead or alive or lying in the street injured and needing help. They were helpless and felt tortured. They had been through a traumatic event, and they felt that they almost lost their son. Jacoby could understand this and it lessened his anger aimed at his mother and father. His parents also understood that they couldn't continue to keep such close tabs on him, that it wasn't good for any of them.

What can survivors tell close friends and family members after a traumatic experience?

Parents want to protect their children; husbands want to protect their wives; wives want to protect their husbands; partners want to protect their partners; children want to protect their parents; siblings want to protect their siblings; friends want to protect their friends. This is natural. This desire to protect extends to not wanting to give loved ones bad news or tell them anything that will upset them. When someone experiences a traumatic event, it can be difficult to know exactly what to say to the loved one. This is not a conversation anyone wants to have.

It is important for trauma survivors to share what happened to them, but it is also important to sometimes measure how much is shared. We advise trauma survivors to share enough that their loved ones can understand what happened to them, what's happening now, and what they need so that the loved ones can support the survivor. Thinking about what level of detail the survivor wants or needs to share prior to talking with someone about trauma details can be helpful. This requires thinking a bit about what is the goal of sharing trauma details with this person at this time.

How much to share with friends and family depends on the person and the trauma survivor's relationship with them. We think it is very important to say aloud all the details of the traumatic event to another person who is trying to be helpful and to do this repeatedly, over and over, as the trauma survivor is processing and trying to make sense of what happened. Some trauma survivors prefer to do this in the context of a professional therapeutic relationship, whereas others prefer to work with their community of family, friends, or others (such as clergy). We know that avoiding thinking and talking about what happened is how PTSD festers, so we encourage sharing. However, we recognize that not everyone can handle hearing about this. If the details of what happened overwhelm the friends or family members and they themselves have a big distressing reaction, then the trauma survivor can be in the position of trying to help and support them. If the friends or family members seem to be haunted by what happened to the trauma survivor, they may need to seek professional help for themselves. If the trauma survivor has a bad reaction after sharing what happened, such as feeling they overwhelmed a friend or family member or regretting that they said anything at all, this may make it less likely that he or she trusts another person enough to tell them what happened.

How much to tell depends on how much friends and family can handle. Sometimes it is best for the survivor to start slow and give the overview of what happened to test the waters. It is not reasonable to expect that friends and family members will have no reaction or not be upset that this happened to their loved one, so the survivor has to expect and allow this expression of emotion. If this is someone who the survivor thinks can help support them, it might be important to share more details of what happened.

If a trauma survivor is not sure how much a friend or family member can handle, it might be best to start with telling a professional what happened and allowing the professional to help figure out who and what to tell. The professional can also help the survivor frame his message, maybe including how he wants the other person to respond. Here are some possible ways to frame this conversation with a friend or family member:

- "I want to tell you what happened, but I'm not ready to answer any questions about it. So can you just let me say what I have to say and leave it at that for now, please?
- "I want to tell you what happened, but I'm not sure how much you want to hear. I will start with the bare bones, but if you want to know more, just ask me."
- "I want to tell you what happened, but I'm sure I will cry. Please don't get upset when I cry."
- "I'm counting on you to let me know if you don't want to hear this or hear the details."
- "I want you to know what happened, but I'm not ready for others to know, so I need you to promise me that you will keep this to yourself."

- "I want you to know what happened, but I think it will make you [angry/scared/worried]. Please try not to have a big reaction when I tell you."

These are just some examples. The point is that the survivor can let their support person know what they need and don't need when they disclose.

We hear from combat Veterans that they don't want their friends and family members to lose their innocence as they have, so they want to protect them from the gory or evil details.

Such Veterans are often reluctant to share details, especially that they've killed someone. This becomes even harder to share if the killing involved civilians or women or children. Rape survivors are often scared to tell exactly what the perpetrator did to them or made them do, such as perform oral or anal sex or say they liked it and wanted it or loved him. Adult survivors of childhood sexual abuse have often carried their secrets for so many years and might even believe what the perpetrator told them such as it was their fault, they wanted it, or the perpetrator would kill or harm their family members if they told. Interpersonal violence survivors are often so ashamed and feel guilty and to blame for their situation and can't imagine that others wouldn't blame them too. Trauma survivors don't want others to see them as they may be seeing themselves. They don't want others to think less of them.

This is why it is so important to tell people who love the trauma survivor what happened. As we discuss throughout this book, supportive and nonjudgmental friends and family members can help so much. A father telling his son that he was also a war Veteran and understands how it happened, that he understands the context of war and knows his son and what kind of person he is, and that he is so sorry his son was faced with that life and death decision but that he is glad his son did what he needed to do for him and his comrades to survive can be so healing.

A mother telling her daughter after a sexual assault that it wasn't her fault, no matter what the perpetrator said, can help so much. A sister telling her sister who is stuck in an abusive marriage that it isn't her fault and that she will do anything her abused sister needs to help, can relieve shame. A friend confiding to a close friend that he was the victim of childhood sexual abuse by his priest and actually felt special can get the support he needs and hear the words that a child can never consent to sexual activity, and of course he felt special, that was what the priest intended; this fact doesn't change the friend's opinion of him except of how strong he is to have survived and carried the burden alone for so long.

Does exercise help?

Exercise, especially regular aerobic exercise, is as effective at reducing mild depression as is antidepressant medication. Exercise is not a treatment for PTSD, but it does help in managing stress, building up stamina, maintaining physical health, and usually improving mood. We recommend whatever the guidelines are. In 2018, the revised federal guidelines suggest that adults should do at least 150 minutes up to 300 minutes a week of moderate-intensity, or 75 minutes up to 150 minutes a week of vigorous-intensity aerobic physical activity or an equivalent combination of moderate- and vigorous-intensity aerobic activity. They should also do muscle-strengthening activities on 2 or more days a week. Exercising outside has the double benefit of exercise and the refreshing effect of being in nature.

What are other services that aren't actual treatment?

We discuss treatments that have been shown to help with PTSD in Chapter 4 of this volume. Many services are available to trauma survivors that are not necessarily treatment. Rape crisis centers may offer support groups. Support is important, but it is not treatment. For active duty military service members, services may be available in military adjustment units. These services may or may not be treatment. Chaplains, medics, first sergeants, and family services can all be useful, but are not treatment. Most Vet centers and VA hospitals offer both treatment and other supportive services that are not treatment. Churches, synagogues, mosques, and other houses of worship may offer spiritual support which is very helpful, but again, is not treatment.

Is there such thing as needing to be ready for treatment?

As mental health professionals who have been working with trauma survivors for over 20 years, we would say that trauma survivors with PTSD are "ready" when they show up at the office saying they want help. Our job is then to provide a good assessment and get them to the most effective treatment as quickly as possible. PTSD is a disorder of avoidance, and any barrier or obstacle or even delay in care will result in many trauma survivors going back to the familiar pattern of avoidance. Assessment aims to get a picture of how they are experiencing PTSD as well as getting a good impression of their full life context and issues that may feed into their PTSD or be relevant to treatment. Once we know that PTSD is present and that PTSD is the issue that needs attention and treatment first (that is, the survivor is not imminently suicidal or using substances to the point where their physical health is in danger), we want to start PTSD-focused effective treatment (psychotherapy or medication) immediately. We want to ensure we are providing a safe and judgment-free environment from the start so that the trauma survivor can feel comfortable to disclose their most difficult memories and difficult thoughts.

For providers who do not have experience working with PTSD or those without experience using effective treatments such as prolonged exposure or cognitive processing therapy, there can be a tendency to want to wait for survivors to say they are ready or to wait for time when there aren't other crises in survivors' lives. For most trauma survivors, emotions are intense. That is part of PTSD! In addition, life can be chaotic with PTSD as people around the survivor may trigger PTSD symptoms. Relationship issues are common as living with someone with PTSD can be difficult in many ways. Having PTSD actually contributes to additional experience of trauma for many survivors.

Most people with PTSD have experienced multiple traumas. Some of these even occur after PTSD has developed. For instance, people with PTSD have negative impacts on their ability to work as a result of the PTSD and are more likely to live in higher crime areas as a result. In practice, when providers wait for survivors to be "ready," this can lead to survivors never having the chance to access effective treatment for PTSD. Instead, providing quick access to collaborative care where the provider and survivor are consistently focused on treatment targets, such as PTSD or depression, allows survivors to quickly engage in care at the moment when motivation is highest. Once they engage in effective care and start to experience benefit, it is much more likely they will continue in care and have an adequate dose of therapy or medication to improve. In addition, allowing for quick access to treatment that recognizes that some people may have a pattern of multiple attempts to start before they actually "stick" can provide an environment that allows the most trauma survivors with PTSD access to effective care.

As previously mentioned, PTSD is a disorder of avoidance. Therefore, the tendency of people with PTSD is to avoid reminders of the trauma and talking about the trauma, and this can also include avoiding treatment. Most psychotherapy is provided in weekly appointments. There is a high dropout from treatment for PTSD as survivors slip back into their avoidant patterns in between sessions. We have some models for PTSD treatment that include daily sessions that help survivors overcome this tendency to avoid that we will talk about in Chapter 4 of this volume. The trauma survivor is urged to fight this tendency to avoid and to ask help from friends, family members, and professionals, for example, by telling them, "I feel I won't want to talk about this again, but I know I need to, so please don't let me off the hook."

How soon after the trauma should a survivor wait to get treatment?

PTSD is only diagnosed if it has been at least 1 month following the traumatic event and the person is experiencing the PTSD symptoms we describe in Chapter 3 of this volume. Therefore, "official" treatment for PTSD would wait until at least 1 month after the trauma when PTSD can be diagnosed. However, we have tried to emphasize that talking about it, thinking about it, writing about it, and getting social support are helpful right away.

What type of early intervention did Lucia receive in the ER?

Lucia was brought to the emergency room where we were conducting a study of an early intervention to try to prevent the development of PTSD, so our study team approached her and asked if she wanted to participate. When her husband, Nick, heard that it might prevent the development of PTSD, he encouraged Lucia to enroll. After describing the study, Lucia consented to participate in the study, so the therapist providing the intervention asked preliminary questions, and then Lucia was officially signed up to participate in the study.

Lucia began the pretreatment assessment approximately 3 hours after the crash. She reported prior trauma including a nonsexual assault by a stranger and by a previous boyfriend, a rating of "near death" for her current trauma severity, and a rating of "somewhat" for her current trauma peritraumatic dissociation (feeling out of touch and like things aren't real). Lucia selected the highest severity response to feeling helpless, horrified, terrified, and out of control during the motor vehicle crash that brought her into the emergency room. *She did not meet criteria for PTSD at any time in her lifetime from the prior assaults or current depression. She reported current minimal depressive symptoms.*

Treatment in the ER

Treatment was the therapy that we described earlier in this chapter in which trauma survivors are asked to tell the story of what just happened, repeatedly, in the present tense, while the therapist records this for the survivor to listen to for homework. Her therapist had Lucia begin her narrative before the first impact and describe everything that was happening in the present tense, including everything that she felt, heard, smelled, and thought. Lucia completed three repetitions of her traumatic event narrative for a total of 44 minutes in the ER. The session data showed a decrease in Lucia's subjective distress from pre-exposure to postexposure (from before her first recounting of the trauma experience to after the final recounting) using a zero to 100 scale where zero mean no distress and 100 means the worst distress imaginable. Her skin conductance (SC; sweatiness of palms) was measured during this process by two little sensors attached with Velcro to two of her fingers. Her SC increased during each imaginal exposure (retelling of the trauma experience) compared to baseline levels (when she was not directly discussing the trauma), but the peak in SC decreased over the course of each imaginal exposure and was lower than baseline at the end of treatment. Lucia's SC matched a typical pattern: During the first recounting, she went through what happened very quickly, and her SC increased a bit from baseline. Her therapist asked her to slow down and report every detail in the second recounting so that it took longer. Her SC increased and stayed elevated much of this recounting, but then was reduced by the end. In her third recounting, her SC did not get as high and came down quickly to below where it was when she started.

Following the recounting, Lucia and the therapist discussed the emotional material that came out during the narrative. Lucia identified effective coping strategies that she used during the trauma, as she was able to transition her fears of dying to thoughts of being "hopeful" and "grateful" while she was riding in the ambulance. She was again scared that she had been seriously injured in the ambulance and feared she would be paralyzed, but she remembered wiggling her toes and fingers in the ambulance and taking that as a good sign. She remembered the EMT's kind words and tone telling her they were just treating her as if she could have spinal injuries as a precaution and she thought Lucia would be fine. She also incorporated the results of the X-ray that showed no spinal injury and the report of the doctor and nurse that she would be sore for a few days but should be fine.

Lucia was able to generate positive self-statements related to the fact that she survived the situation and believed that good things would come out of the crash, such as her being more responsible and caring of others. She was happy that she wasn't pregnant at the time as she would have worried about the baby. Additionally, although she felt anger toward the truck driver, she made the decision to focus on the kindness and helpfulness of the bystanders and paramedics, a part of the trauma that became more evident to her as she was going through the imaginal exposure.

The therapist and Lucia created a list of behavioral exposures to be completed over the coming weeks. The policewoman thought that Lucia's car was probably going to be considered "totaled" by the insurance company, so she was likely going to have to get a new car. In the meantime, the truck driver's insurance would probably supply her with a rental car. In response to Lucia feeling hesitant to resume her normal driving routine, Lucia and her therapist created a plan in which Lucia agreed to first complete less anxiety-provoking exposures such as sitting in the driver's seat with the car turned off and driving around her neighborhood side streets. They constructed a plan to get her driving by herself back to the school where she taught within a week. Lucia identified doing yoga and spending time with her family as self-care activities and agreed to take the following day as a sick day from work to give herself time to recover and process what happened.

Follow-up assessments

One month after the crash, Lucia had a follow-up assessment with the therapist, in which Lucia reported mild PTSD symptoms, but she did not meet criteria for PTSD. She was hypervigilant while driving and easily startled, especially while driving. She thought about the crash at least a few times a week and was still nervous when driving, especially in the rain. The SC data indicated no increase in her body's physical stress level as measured by the sweatiness of her palms in response to talking about what happened at the 1-month follow-up. Lucia reported very minimal depressive symptoms that were not significantly different from how she had been feeling before the crash.

At her 3-month follow-up, Lucia continued to report the same mild PTSD symptoms particularly around driving. She did not meet criteria for PTSD, her minimal depressive symptoms were not significantly different from her pretreatment and 1-month follow-up reports, and she did not show an increase in SC in response to trauma reminders. Lucia reported no avoidance of driving the same highway to work, no avoidance of thinking about or talking about the crash, and that she knew it would take time to reduce her hypervigilance and startle when driving. She credited the early intervention for helping her, as she could imagine having wanted to avoid driving if the therapist hadn't encouraged her not to avoid in the ER. She also liked the reframing of some of her scary thoughts that she was going to die or be seriously injured to being grateful that she was alive and focusing on the kindness others showed her.

3

WHAT IS PTSD?

As we discussed in Chapter 2 of this book, experiencing a traumatic event is like going through the grief process. We need to emotionally process the painful emotions. There is no way to the other side of the pain except through it. But many people with posttraumatic stress disorder (PTSD) don't process it. They avoid the pain. It festers, and this is how it haunts them. While each trauma survivor will experience PTSD in his or her own way, there are common symptoms of PTSD.

What are the symptoms of PTSD?

Next we discuss four groups (also known as "clusters") of PTSD symptoms. These groups are

- Intrusive symptoms,
- Avoidance symptoms,
- Negative mood symptoms (negative alterations in thoughts and mood), and
- Hyperarousal symptoms (alterations in physical arousal and reactivity).

Within the four clusters, there are 20 symptoms of PTSD.

Intrusive symptoms

When someone is haunted by something that happened to her in her past, common symptoms that can happen day or night include *nightmares, flashbacks,* and *physical reminders* in the body. The haunting nature comes out in the re-experiencing symptoms of PTSD. These are sometimes called the intrusive symptoms because they pop into the minds of people suffering from PTSD and interfere with whatever they are doing in the moment. Intrusive symptoms are the first cluster of symptoms that make up PTSD. These symptoms often make survivors feel like they are going crazy or like they are out of control. How much these intrusions interfere with a person's life varies from person to person. They can change day to day or even based on what part of the trauma memory pops into the survivor's mind. You've probably heard of war Veterans who hear a car backfire and hit the ground or a child who has been repeatedly beaten flinch when an adult raises a hand just to brush back the child's hair. These are clear examples of re-experiencing or intrusive symptoms.

Intrusive symptoms include when images of the trauma memory come back or even when the person thinks about the trauma and then feels strong emotions or has physical reactions. Intrusive symptoms include nightmares where survivors may have parts of the trauma memory replay in their dreams or the nightmares may be a variation of the trauma memory or a similar situation. For instance, rape survivors may have intense dreams of being attacked or chased, dreams that are not exactly what happened but produce the same emotional reactions.

Cynthia had dreams of being attacked and pushed to the ground where she thought she was being smothered and then she would wake up. These dreams happened at least five times per week, and she would wake up in a sweat and sometimes screaming. Most days after she woke up, Cynthia was not able to get back to sleep. Thomas's nightmares almost always involved fires. Sometimes they were a replay of the improvised explosive device (IED) event, and other times he would be having a normal unrelated dream and then fire would start and it would switch to the IED. He would thrash around in his sleep almost every night and woke up from these dreams at least four or five times each week. Thomas found that if he had a shot of bourbon when he woke up, he could often get back to sleep for at least a bit. This habit contributed to his increasing drinking as the nightmares got worse.

Examples of PTSD we see in the media often show a trauma survivor who has some type of trauma reminder and then loses touch with the current situation and reacts as though the trauma is actually happening again. This PTSD symptom is called a flashback. While this is a very vivid example of how some survivors experience their haunting memories, true flashbacks mean that the survivor loses touch with the fact that he is in the present and feels like he is reliving the past, even if just for a moment. Such experiences are much less common in PTSD than you may believe. In addition, such flashbacks are typically short-lived, with the survivor realizing that he is no longer in the trauma within a minute or two. Even though they are rare, when a flashback happens, it is often terrifying for the trauma survivor and leads to a real sense that he is going crazy or becoming out of control.

Cynthia experienced a flashback when her boyfriend, Scott, came to her apartment the week after the rape. She had been avoiding him, and he finally just showed up at her door asking if they could talk. Cynthia let him in because she felt horrible that she had not spoken to him since the night of the rape. She wanted to tell him what had happened, but she also did not want to start crying again. So she said that she just had too many assignments and had not been able to do anything but work and school. Scott reached out to hug Cynthia, but as soon as his arms were around her she had a flashback to when her attacker was on top of her on the bed. She let out a yelp and pushed Scott away. He stepped back in surprise, and she said he needed to leave now. She would talk with him later, and she would explain then. Scott looked confused and hurt, and Cynthia felt horrible, but she also did not feel like she knew Scott well enough to tell him in that moment. They had been dating for less than 2 months when the rape happened. She just was not ready to tell him about what happened or to risk anything. She did not want to start crying again as she felt she was barely holding onto control as it was.

Sometimes, the intrusive symptoms are felt in the survivor's body. There is no blood test or stress test that can confirm yet if someone has PTSD. But some *symptoms* of PTSD can be measured by looking at physical information, such as our heart rate, skin conductance (how sweaty our skin is), and acoustic startle response (how jumpy we are when we hear a sound). When survivors with PTSD are reminded of the trauma, their bodies tend to react to these triggers more than do people who don't have PTSD. Some studies have found that people with PTSD can be more reactive overall (increased heart rate when reminded), and can have a harder time turning off the reactivity when it is turned on (takes longer to calm down), and their physical reactivity is more sensitive to reminders than people without PTSD (things that are only remotely connected to the trauma may set the whole system to react, such as seeing a man who is physically similar to the rapist). Many other areas of medicine use biomarkers to help make a diagnosis. Biomarkers are ways of looking at what's going on in the body such as fever, blood tests, X-rays, computed tomography scans, and electrocardiograms. Figuring out the best biomarkers to help us identify PTSD is an important area for continued research in PTSD.

Avoidance symptoms

While there are different theories about how PTSD develops, we are certain that avoidance is what keeps someone from recovering. Avoidance is the second cluster of PTSD symptoms. Avoidance for most trauma survivors starts as they retreat to their safe places to recover following a trauma, but then they never get back to their usual daily lives because it feels to them that what was previously considered safe is no longer safe. Avoidance is one big way that trauma survivors' lives are taken away by PTSD. Survivors who begin to feel that they can no longer do the things that matter to them or accomplish the things that make them a functioning adult, quickly feel a sense of failure and incompetence. Such feelings feed the avoidance, and their lives get smaller and smaller as they continue to avoid. Avoidance is always a critical piece of PTSD no matter the type of trauma. Avoidance is the engine that drives the PTSD symptoms to intrude on a survivor's functioning more and more over time.

When Thomas got home from the hospital after his deployment, his family was so happy to have him home. They had prepared the house for his return based on the suggestions of the rehabilitation case manager. Christine and the kids were very excited to see him and have him home. But Thomas felt immediately overwhelmed by the people and attention, and he retreated to his room. Christine and their two daughters, Cary and Sarah, were sad that he did not want to spend time with them. He would only come out of his room for meals and to watch football games. When he did come out, he was angry and his face was puffy from crying and drinking. Christine invited a few of his military friends over for a playoff football game. Thomas had agreed to this visit, but on the day of the game he smiled only a little, barely talked to anyone, and drank too much. Thomas was avoiding his family, his military friends, and going out. This avoidance was so severe that he became quite depressed, and his drinking to cope with intrusive symptoms made the depression worse. Avoidance of the memory and the people, places, and situations related to the IED incident left Thomas stuck and sad.

Veterans might be more emotionally avoidant than other PTSD sufferers. They are trained to disengage from their emotions—a good thing if you're in a war zone; you don't want to have a big emotional reaction in a combat zone. So they put their emotions in a box and try to keep it locked. But then once they come home, they can still be disengaged from their emotions. This is not a good thing for being able to participate fully in life, feeling close to family and friends, and emotionally processing traumatic events. This same pattern of disengaging from emotion to accomplish a job can also occur in police and other first responders.

Negative mood symptoms

The third cluster of PTSD symptoms is called negative alterations in thoughts and mood." *As we previously described with Thomas, the more he avoided, the worse he felt about himself and his ability to handle the world. He felt more and more depressed and saw each time he avoided as further proof that he was a flawed person.* These negative thoughts about the self and world are part of PTSD. Trauma survivors will often report feeling that they reacted poorly at the time of the trauma in either things they did or did not do and that they somehow brought the trauma on themselves or made it worse, despite the evidence that they performed just fine.

Thomas went over and over in his head how he "missed" the IED and that he must have been tired and not paying enough attention. He felt that he had failed his unit by not avoiding the IED. In addition, Thomas now felt that with his injured leg, he was vulnerable to the dangerous world where people are always trying to take advantage of you or hurt you. He felt unable to protect Christine and the kids and unable to lead his crew at work. The more Thomas felt incompetent, the more hopeless and helpless he felt.

Hyperarousal symptoms

The last PTSD symptom cluster is known as "alterations in physical arousal and reactivity." We previously discussed that arousal and reactivity can be triggered by reminders of the trauma as part of the intrusive symptoms. PTSD also results in a general sense of constantly being on edge and a sense of constantly needing to be ready for bad things to happen. People with PTSD often feel there is danger lurking around every corner, and this comes out in hyperarousal symptoms.

This general sense of threat is the hyperarousal and reactivity cluster of PTSD.

For example, people with PTSD have problems sleeping. You may remember that nightmares are a part of intrusive symptoms, but people with PTSD often have general problems falling and/or staying asleep in addition to problems caused by nightmares. They will often talk about not wanting to go to sleep for fear of having nightmares or even not being able to turn off their brain to go to sleep as they are thinking so much about what happened or are just not able to shut it down. Many people with PTSD feel vulnerable while asleep, and so they find it hard to relax and get to sleep. If you are scared, nighttime can be a very scary time: The house is dark, everyone is asleep, and if someone is hypervigilant, it is very easy to misinterpret normal night noises. They overreact to the slightest noise, worrying that there is an intruder in the house and having defensive thoughts about how they will protect themselves and their families, and all of this wrecks their sleep.

People with PTSD want to be very aware of everything in their environment; we call this "hypervigilance." They often report that they constantly check for signs of safety. This checking can occur at home where people with PTSD may find that they check and recheck the locks or they increase security around their home following trauma. Hypervigilance often occurs when people go out, and they only go to places that they have previously checked out to ensure they have certain security measures in place. It may include only going out to certain stores and certain times of day when the crowds are less.

Cynthia would only go to the grocery store when Judy could go with her because Cynthia was afraid of coming home and having someone follow her as she feared had happened the night of the rape. When she was at the store, she would notice all the security cameras and think about where she would run if someone approached her. She worried that the attacker, who was never identified or caught, was going to come back and approach her either at home or when she ventured out from her apartment.

Christine thought it would be good for Thomas to get out of the house and go grocery shopping with her and the girls. She noticed that he was constantly scanning their surroundings, wouldn't let the girls out of his sight, and would look left and right before they could round the corner to go down a new aisle. Thomas was essentially pulling guard duty trying to protect his family due to his PTSD. All of these actions are part of hypervigilance in PTSD.

What are the DSM and ICD?

The clusters of PTSD symptoms as previously described are part of the American Psychiatric Association's *Diagnostic and Statistical Manual* (DSM).[1] The fifth edition, known as the DSM-5, is the most common system of psychiatric diagnoses in the United States. The categories and symptoms have been developed and revised over many years. PTSD was first included as a diagnosis in the third edition (DSM-III) in 1980. Every several years, the American Psychiatric Association decides whether revision of the DSM is needed and then convenes researchers and experts to determine what changes if any are needed. The proposed changes are then put forward to the field for review and feedback, and then a final revision is collated and published for use. Over time the symptoms that make up the diagnosis of PTSD have changed from the DSM-III to the current DSM-5. These changes try to describe PTSD more precisely and make sure that the diagnosis helps people with PTSD get diagnosed and then find appropriate treatment.

The World Health Organization has also developed a system of categorization and diagnosis of all physical and mental health conditions called the *International Statistical Classification of Diseases and Related Health Problems* (ICD), which is now in its 11th revision (ICD-11). This system is used widely throughout the world, and PTSD symptoms are described slightly differently in ICD-11 and DSM-5. However, the main idea in both volumes is that PTSD represents a stuck memory of a life threatening traumatic experience that haunts the survivor in intrusive symptoms and avoidance.

How can you tell the difference between chronic grief and PTSD?

The response to trauma is similar to the grief process, and there is no getting to the other side except through the pain. Sometimes PTSD involves actual grief, especially when someone died, but also for the loss of innocence. People with PTSD often think that those who haven't experienced trauma are naïve and that they don't know what a dangerous world this is.

Grief is a normal reaction when we lose someone we love. For most of us, by fully experiencing that grief such as through crying, thinking about the person, talking about the person, and missing the person, the grief gradually lessens over time. We will always miss the person we lost, and it will always be sad, but the pain can lessen; for example, we may be able to think about them 6 months later without crying. This is the normal pattern of grief.

Sometimes this pattern gets disrupted, especially if someone doesn't allow themselves to fully experience these painful emotions. It can also be disrupted if circumstances don't allow this process, such as fleeing a war or disaster zone or caring for the surviving injured. Similar to PTSD, if the survivor doesn't properly grieve for the lost person, it can fester and haunt them. The treatment for grief is very similar to the treatment for PTSD and usually involves exposure to painful memories, reminders, and objects to allow the grief process to proceed.

Especially when there is a loss of life involved in a traumatic event, grief is intertwined with PTSD. Sometimes the trauma survivor may not want to get better on some level as they think this might mean that they would forget the person who didn't survive. Sometimes they feel guilty that they survived and others did not. Most PTSD therapists are trained to help with these thoughts that are sometimes referred to as "survivor's guilt." Treatment includes discussion about honoring the deceased person's memory and that not getting better is not the way to honor their memory. In fact, the best way to honor their memory is to live fully. What would the deceased person say to the survivor if they could? What if it was the other way around? What would the trauma survivor tell the deceased person? In all cases, the survivor understands that the deceased person would tell them to go on and live their life. We also remind the trauma survivor that they couldn't forget the deceased person if they tried, and we are not asking them to forget.

What are some other non-PTSD problems that can develop after a trauma?

While some people develop PTSD following trauma, this is not the only possible negative mental health consequence of trauma. For some people, other mental health issues begin following trauma and can range across the spectrum of issues. Indeed, for many, the stress of trauma may trigger a risk for certain mental health concerns that may not have come up if trauma did not occur. For others, they may develop these other mental health issues at the same time as the PTSD.

Depression

One common mental health issue that can develop alone or in combination with PTSD is depression. Depression is an overwhelming sense of sadness and worthlessness that pervades the survivor's life for at least 2 weeks and often longer. Depression symptoms include loss of interest and sadness, loss of appetite or increased appetite, low energy, and sleep problems. People who are depressed often report sleeping too much or not sleeping at all and trouble starting activities or accomplishing tasks. They tend to have a general sense of worthlessness and loss of hope for things to change in the future. They may even have thoughts about hurting themselves. Of importance, there are effective treatment options for depression. For example, several medications have shown to be effective in reducing depression. In addition, several types of therapy, including cognitive-behavioral therapy, behavioral activation, and interpersonal therapy are effective in reducing depression. For some people with depression as their primary problem, there will be periods of relapse over time even with effective treatment. Mindfulness-based cognitive therapy has been shown to reduce the frequency of such relapses over time for people who have initially responded well to many depression treatments (both medications and psychotherapies).

There is some overlap in PTSD and depression that can contribute to the high rates of co-occurrence of these problems in trauma survivors. As mentioned previously, problems with sleep, loss of interest, and a sense of worthlessness or self-blame for bad things happening all directly overlap between PTSD and depression. Across PTSD treatment studies, over half of people with PTSD also were clinically depressed. For most patients with both of these mental health concerns, the depression improves as the PTSD is treated. In such cases, we think the depression most likely developed out of an increased sense of hopelessness following the trauma and reaction to the PTSD symptoms themselves. This makes sense since having PTSD is difficult and not being able to do the things you want because you are afraid of a trauma from your past is frustrating. It makes sense that a person experiencing PTSD over time may become depressed that they are not able to do what they want to do in their life. It also makes sense that as they engage in treatment and begin to see that they *can* do those things they want to do again, they may see their depression improve as well.

Panic disorder

Panic disorder may also develop following trauma. Just as with depression, panic may develop alongside PTSD or on its own without PTSD. Panic attacks are when your body has a rapidly increasing intense physical reaction. For most people this includes racing heart, a feeling of blood pumping fast, feeling that they can't catch their breath, and a sense that they may be having a heart attack or dying. It may also include digestive symptoms. Such attacks are common and on their own are not considered a mental health issue. Almost everyone has a panic attack at some point in their lives. Such attacks become panic disorder if the attacks come seemingly out of the blue, and we respond to the attack with extreme fear of having another attack and therefore change our behavior to prevent or avoid another attack or minimize the consequences of having such an attack.

For instance, Gary attended church one Sunday; in the middle of the service he felt his heart racing and he thought he was having a heart attack. He had to push people out of his way to get out of the pew and was mortified that people saw him react in this way. After he stepped out to the bathroom, the reaction subsided, and he was embarrassed and never wanted that to happen again. He then decided that he would only go to church from now on if his son could go with him and *he will only stay at the service if he can get a seat on the outside of the pew. So, Gary had a panic attack at church. He responded with extreme fear over the consequences of the attack and whether he would have another attack* and *he changed his behavior to lessen his sense that he might have another attack or the consequences of an attack if it occurs.*

People with panic disorder often restrict their lives in an attempt to try and prevent attacks, and they end up afraid of people, places, and situations that are actually safe. They end up having a sense that they cannot live their life or do the things that they want or need to do because they are so afraid of having a panic attack. Often people suffering with panic disorder rush to the emergency room only to find out that they are not having a heart attack or any physical issues.

In a person with PTSD, panic attacks can be part of the PTSD. Specifically, if they have panic attacks only in response to trauma reminders or PTSD symptoms, then we would include those panic attacks within the PTSD diagnosis and not add a panic disorder diagnosis. An independent panic disorder diagnosis would occur if the attacks are not in response to trauma reminders, the survivor is afraid of the consequences of the attacks, and he changes his behavior to try and prevent or avoid the attack itself. Panic attacks in response to PTSD triggers typically respond well to the PTSD treatment without any modification. If panic attacks not in response to trauma triggers are occurring and the survivor is changing his behaviors to prevent or avoid the consequences of panic attacks, then adding additional panic specific treatment may be warranted.

Medications for both panic disorder and PTSD are available. If the survivor is engaging in PTSD-specific psychotherapy, often the panic disorder can be combined in the same treatment course. For instance, in the case of Gary, his first panic attack at church that was previously described occurred after a severe physical assault that occurred when he was walking home from work one evening. Following the attack, he took several weeks off of work and now only takes a cab to and from work. He blamed himself for the attack and felt like a weak person. Over this month since his physical attack, he developed PTSD and the panic disorder as previously noted. If he was engaging in prolonged exposure, the therapist could incorporate psychoeducation about avoidance as it relates to the trauma memory and now the panic attack and then could establish exposures to address both issues at the same time. Gary could have on his hierarchy items such as walking to work on his own (neighborhood is generally safe and others typically walk to work) that targets the trauma avoidance and feeling his heart racing as an exposure targeting the panic attack symptoms that he avoids.

Obsessive compulsive disorder

Obsessive compulsive disorder (OCD) can also develop or increase in severity following trauma. OCD includes obsessions and compulsions. *Obsessions* are thoughts that come back repeatedly and that cause significant anxiety and fear. *Compulsions* are thoughts or behaviors that the person engages in to attempt to reduce or prevent the anxiety from the obsession or to feel "just right." This cycle of obsessions and reacting with compulsions occurs with a frequency and severity that it interferes with the ability of the person to accomplish their daily tasks. For trauma survivors who have OCD prior to trauma, the frequency and intensity of obsessions and compulsions often increases (at least temporarily) from what it was prior to the trauma. For trauma survivors without OCD prior to trauma, OCD can develop on its own following trauma, or it may develop at the same time as PTSD. For example, some rape survivors have told us they feel dirty following the assault and wash themselves compulsively. Some combat veterans have reported repeatedly checking door and window locks, especially before bedtime. As with panic disorder and PTSD, medications for both OCD and PTSD are often the same with variation in combinations or dosage. Psychotherapy for both PTSD and OCD can often be combined. In severe cases, specific focused and separate episodes of care for each disorder may be warranted, and additional sessions to ensure there is time for full-focused treatment of both issues is often necessary.

Let's consider the case of Zaniya, who had OCD as a young girl. At that time, her primary obsession revolved around wanting things to be "just right," or she felt like something bad would happen and her mother would die. She would spend hours arranging and rearranging her bathroom drawers to have things straight. She always had to have her pencils in a specific way in her desk. Her OCD was relatively mild, and when her teacher told Zaniya's parents about how these behaviors were interfering with her finishing her work, the child

*was started on a medication that was quite effective. She stopped the
medication at age 10 and has not had a return of symptoms.*

*At 15, Zaniya was sexually assaulted by her friend Karen's older
brother at a birthday party for Karen. She did not tell anyone about
what happened and quit engaging in any social activities. She started
straightening things again and arranging and rearranging items in
her bathroom drawers. This time she was thinking she needed to keep
things just right to prevent bad things from happening to her. She
blamed herself for the rape because she had had a crush on Karen's
brother, and when he was paying attention to her, she was so excited
and wanted to spend time alone with him. However, as soon as they
were alone, he raped her. She yelled, but the other people at the party
did not hear her over the music. Her friend Karen had no idea what
had happened when she did not return.*

*In this case, Zaniya saw a return of the OCD symptoms with
a slight change—she was afraid for her own safety instead of her
mother's. The frequency of the obsessions and compulsions was interfering with her life. In addition to the OCD, Zaniya was pushing
thoughts of the rape out of her head; blaming herself for what happened; and avoiding people, places, and situations that related to the
rape. She had PTSD. In this case, exposure-based psychotherapy to
address both OCD and PTSD may be a good course of action.*

Social anxiety disorder

Social anxiety disorder may also develop following trauma
and can occur with PTSD or on its own. Social anxiety disorder occurs when a person avoids or endures with significant distress social interactions or situations where social
interactions may occur, out of a fear of negative evaluation
or an inflated sense that someone might have a negative reaction. For trauma survivors who had social anxiety prior to
trauma, their social anxiety symptoms may worsen at least
temporarily. If the trauma was interpersonal, such as a rape,
the social anxiety disorder may show even more increase. For
survivors who did not have social anxiety disorder prior to

trauma, the social anxiety disorder may develop on its own or in combination with PTSD. If the social concerns are all related to fear that the trauma may happen again (such as fear in crowds), then the additional social anxiety disorder diagnosis would not be provided, but if the survivor has separate social concerns and avoidance related to people negatively evaluating them, then the additional diagnosis would be provided and treatment focused on those concerns would be warranted.

Let's consider Kerry, who experienced a severe industrial accident at work. Following the accident, Kerry was in the hospital for a week as they worked to set his injuries and heal enough for him to go home. Kerry could not drive for several months due to his badly broken leg. He noticed that he was avoiding getting into cars again, so decided to intentionally take extra trips with his dad to get out of the house and be in cars. Over the weeks that followed, it got easier, and when he got the cast off, he was ready to drive and be independent again. However, when Kerry returned to work he noticed that he was shying away from people, and when he was asked to speak about the accident and his related experiences during a work meeting, he started feeling very anxious. He made his presentation but kept stuttering and got red in the face and felt embarrassed after he was done. His coworkers teased him good-naturedly, and this made Kerry even more self-conscious. He was asked to do another talk, this time for management investigating the accident, but he made an excuse as to why he could not do it.

Kerry had never been comfortable with public speaking, but after the accident, he would have lots of physical signs of anxiety in these situations, and he would avoid them as much as he could. He stopped hanging out with lots of people and only had one real friend he kept in touch with. At this point, Kerry appears to have conquered any signs of PTSD, but social anxiety disorder appears to be developing. Both medications and psychotherapy can be effective for treatment of social anxiety disorder.

Specific phobia

Finally, specific phobia, which is fear and avoidance of a specific person, place, or thing that interferes with function, may develop either alone or in combination with PTSD. If the person, place, or thing is related to the trauma, then there would not be an independent specific phobia diagnosis. In these cases, the item would be considered a part of the PTSD and would be part of that treatment plan. Common specific phobias include spider phobia, other insect phobias, snake phobia, or fear of flying or water. While the name "specific phobia" makes it seem like this may not be such a big deal, for some people, the avoidance associated with trying to not have contact with their feared object can be quite intrusive and can prevent them from doing the things they want or need to do.

In the case of James, he was involved in a car accident and did not develop PTSD, but following that incident, he found that he could no longer tolerate airplane travel. He was terrified to get on an airplane. As a traveling speaker, James typically had at least two trips per month. He had been driving since this fear had arisen, but with an increase in travel across coasts, he was having to cancel or not book talks due to his fear of flying. As this began to impact his livelihood, James decided he had to address it head on. Typically, specific phobia treatment involves exposure therapy to flying on actual airplanes or using virtual airplanes if it is virtual reality exposure therapy, and treatment tends to be very effective usually within several sessions.

What about people who have some symptoms but may not meet the full diagnostic criteria for PTSD?

For some people following trauma, they may find that the initial upset gets a little better but never quite goes away. For some, this may lean more toward the memory popping into their minds from time to time but only being moderately upsetting or only rarely popping in. For others, the memory may not be an issue, but they find themselves avoiding people, places, or situations that may remind them of the trauma. Finally, for others, this may be reflected in a constant sense of being on edge and watching for threats in their environment. Each of these situations can be described as "subthreshold PTSD," meaning not quite meeting the full PTSD criteria.

This subthreshold category of posttrauma reactions describes those trauma survivors who have some of the symptoms of PTSD, but the severity and frequency of those symptoms within each of the four clusters of PTSD (intrusion, avoidance, negative thoughts and mood, and hypervigilance) does not reach the threshold for a full diagnosis. If the distress related to these symptoms reaches a level where it interferes with the functioning of the survivor, then a diagnosis may or may not be given, but treatment would be useful. As noted at the start of this chapter, PTSD is defined by 20 symptoms divided into four clusters, so someone may not meet the full diagnostic criteria yet still be suffering and would still profit from treatment. Of note, research supports that the medications and psychotherapies that are effective for full-blown PTSD are also effective for subthreshold PTSD. For psychotherapy, the number of sessions required for a survivor's response to therapy may be reduced. For medications, there may be justification for focusing on primary symptoms (such as sleep disturbance) if the worst symptoms are just in that area.

Does it mean that you are weak if you have PTSD?

No! Many trauma survivors who are suffering with the symptoms of PTSD ponder this question. In fact, worries about having PTSD can actually make those same symptoms grow. The more a survivor feels broken or weak and unable to handle the world, the worse she will become over time. The more she avoids, the less she will be able to function in her life. *PTSD does not mean that a person is weak.* It means that given the specifics of someone's circumstances and experiences at the time of the trauma, the memory got stuck and is now haunting them. This may be due to biology, number or severity of the event, age at the time of the trauma, the meaning attached to the event, or a combination of these factors. In the end, however, research really points to the fact that *anyone under the right combination of factors can end up with PTSD.* In treatment, one of the main goals of the therapist is to provide corrective experiences for the survivor so that they can learn they are strong, they are able to handle upsetting and traumatic events, and their survival is part of the proof of their strength as a person.

Isn't PTSD the "war Veterans' disease?"

As discussed earlier in this book, many people think of PTSD as the "war Veterans' disease." PTSD is certainly a problem for some war Veterans, but as we have already mentioned, PTSD can occur following any type of trauma exposure. With about 70 percent of people experiencing a potentially traumatic event in their lifetimes, PTSD really is a major public health concern. Since PTSD requires a life threatening event to oneself or others, combat is a common traumatic event that leads to PTSD, but most Veterans who experience combat do not develop PTSD or other mental health issues. In fact, many Veterans can relate harrowing tales of their ability to manage difficult and heroic situations in combat and come through it with a sense of accomplishment for what they were able to do as part of their service.

Are there genetic factors that impact PTSD?

Research shows that there are genetic factors that make some people more vulnerable to mental health issues generally and there are genetic factors that make some people more vulnerable to negative consequences following a trauma. However, none of these genetic factors are strong enough that someone with these factors will definitely get PTSD. Instead, each of the genetic markers associated with PTSD interacts with trauma exposure and other environmental factors to increase the risk of developing PTSD symptoms over time.

There is good news about genes and PTSD. Remember Lucia and the study we discussed in Chapters 1 and 2 of this book in which we helped trauma survivors in the emergency room talk about what just happened to them and how this lowered their rates of PTSD by half 3 months later? That early intervention seemed to lessen a genetic risk for PTSD. In fact, for the patients who received the early intervention and had the genetic risk for PTSD, 3 months later looked like the patients who did not have the genetic risk for PTSD. This is eventually what we want to be able to do—identify people who are more at risk for developing PTSD and get them the early intervention to help them *not* develop PTSD.

Are there other risk factors for developing PTSD?

As we have mentioned several times throughout this book, there are many risk factors for developing PTSD, and under the right combination of circumstances, anyone can develop PTSD following trauma. But it is very important not to forget that even with the highest-risk traumas, we see resilience of the human spirit. Those people who are more at risk of developing the symptoms of PTSD following trauma exposure experience more frequent traumas, more severe traumas, and/or trauma during childhood. In addition, survivors experiencing certain types of trauma—specifically those involving interpersonal violence such as sexual assault or physical assault—have higher rates of PTSD than those whose traumas do not involve interpersonal trauma, such as natural disasters.

Finally, risk of having PTSD is greatly increased for survivors who feel that those around them do not support their recovery from the trauma or feel that those around them in some way blame the survivor for the trauma or its consequences.

For Thomas, even though his fellow soldiers came to his
support at the time, he feels that they must blame him for
the loss of his friend, and these feelings weigh heavily on
him. Rather than face people who he feels blamed him,
he withdrew into alcohol and isolation. When Christine
became concerned about his drinking and tried to talk
about this with him, Thomas interpreted this as his wife's
rejecting and criticizing him and what he perceived as
his needs.

For many trauma survivors, what may begin with a poorly
worded comment from a friend, police officer, or other person
following the trauma can take on a life of its own, driving the
survivor to isolate herself and withdraw from life and activities even more.

For instance, while Cynthia was being questioned by a
female police officer during the rape kit examination in
the emergency room, the officer asked if she had locked her
apartment door when she arrived home that night. Later
Cynthia learned that this was because there was a serial
rapist who was following people in the area and that his
way of targeting victims was to find an unlocked door.
The officer was trying to connect the case information.
However, upon hearing this question, Cynthia could not
remember locking the door and, in fact, thought she may
have forgotten as she raced to the bathroom when she first
got home. Cynthia took this as the officer saying that she,
herself, was to blame for her rape.

Keeping this risk in mind, sensitivity and positive regard
without judgment are key when interacting with trauma survivors. Working to ensure that their basic needs are met and
they have a nonjudgmental ear to listen to their experiences
can be therapeutic and really the best thing that we can do to
reduce the risk of PTSD.

What about people who develop PTSD and substance abuse?

For many people suffering with PTSD, alcohol and substance misuse goes hand in hand with PTSD symptoms. Many researchers have investigated the complex relationship between PTSD and alcohol and substance misuse. For some trauma survivors, the alcohol or substance misuse may have occurred before they experienced the trauma that led to PTSD. For others, the misuse or obtaining the substances may have led to being in dangerous situations where the trauma occurred. For instance, someone who is abusing alcohol may become cognitively compromised and may be victimized physically or sexually as a result. For others, the PTSD was already a part of their lives, and they started to use alcohol or other substances to try and push the memory away, or to get to sleep or in some other way deal with the symptoms, or as a way to avoid the memories or symptoms. When this pattern is present, it is called "self-medication." Even for those who started using substances prior to PTSD, they may continue to use or use more often or more intensely to try and manage the symptoms of PTSD.

Consider Brittany, who started drinking alcohol when she was 11. Brittany came from a neglectful home where there was minimal supervision. She had trouble in school and found that kids thought she was funny and cool when she was drinking. She could have parties at her home because her mom worked the night shift. She started drinking more often and inviting older kids to her parties. In the course of a year, Brittany went from drinking once a week to several nights per week. At one of the parties, she passed out on the couch while all her friends were dancing. Brittany awoke to an empty house and a large man who she did not know raping her. She was going in and out of consciousness and crying and screaming. She fully awoke, and he left. The house was empty, and she ran to clean up her body and the house before her mom got home from work.

Over the next several weeks, Brittany continued to drink and have parties. She only told her best friend about what had happened. She was scared to tell any adults for fear of getting into trouble for the parties and drinking. Her friend stayed over at her place most nights. Brittany was drinking every night to pass out and get some sleep. Even with that, she woke up screaming with the image of the man raping her. The nightmares were intense. She was getting very little sleep and most of the sleep was not restful due to alcohol use. She avoided people outside of her parties, and her grades dropped. She was acting out at school, and her mom was called repeatedly to pick her up after Brittany was sleeping through class. One teacher, Ms. Anderson, noticed the change in Brittany's behavior and approached her to ask what was going on. When Ms. Anderson asked what was wrong, Brittany started crying uncontrollably. After an intense discussion, Ms. Anderson contacted Brittany's mother, and they were able to start the young woman on a path for combined alcohol use disorder and PTSD treatment.

Brittany's case shows both how some people have problematic alcohol use prior to trauma exposure and how PTSD symptoms can often lead people to drink more to try and manage the reexperiencing and push the memory out of their thoughts.

Treatment when a trauma survivor has both alcohol or substance use disorder and PTSD can be difficult. Where does treatment start? What works best? It was previously believed that trauma survivors with alcohol or substance use disorder needed to demonstrate a period of abstinence prior to treating the PTSD. However, this often put survivors in a situation where they had a very tough time maintaining abstinence in the face of reexperiencing symptoms and the reexperiencing sometimes gets more intense as the alcohol or substance use is reduced. This is a tough cycle that many survivors could not break, and they ended up never able to access PTSD care as they could not have a long enough period of abstinence to get it.

Over the last 10 years, significant research has been conducted with this population and has demonstrated that the best way to address this comorbidity is to provide simultaneous alcohol/substance use disorder and PTSD treatment. This treatment can occur with separate providers: one who leads the alcohol or substance abuse treatment and one who leads the PTSD treatment. This requires lots of communication between providers but can be very successful since each provider is drawing on their expertise. Another option is to use one of the combined treatment protocols, such as COPE (Concurrent Treatment of PTSD and Substance Use Disorders Using Prolonged Exposure) where a single provider addresses both issues within one treatment.

Trauma survivors suffering with alcohol and substance use disorder and PTSD now have more options for care. Of note, treatment providers will examine what makes the most sense for a given survivor based on the level and type of substance use disorder and the PTSD that he or she is experiencing. For people where safety and physical health are at higher risk or where medical detox is needed, that will need to be addressed first, and a period of stability may be needed prior to moving forward. However, more inpatient substance use disorder settings are integrating trauma-focused care to support trauma survivors at all stages of treatment.

What are the consequences of having PTSD?

PTSD can impact all areas of functioning, including family relationships and work. As we previously discussed in the symptoms of PTSD, the disorder can look different in each person. That being said, the hallmark of PTSD is that *the memory of a life-threatening experience is stuck and haunting the survivor.*

PTSD impacts family relationships. Many people with PTSD feel that they cannot connect with others emotionally.

Good things happen but they don't feel happy. Or things happen to people they used to care about and they react with numbness instead of the joy or sadness that they may have felt before or that they see others feeling around them. For some people with PTSD this results in the breakdown of relationships and even in divorce or loss of child custody. One of the most rewarding experiences that we have as therapists is when a parent who previously did not have a healthy relationship with his or her children reports a new opening of communication as their PTSD symptoms improve, or they even experience a healing and develop the ability to have fun with their kids again. One Vietnam Veteran even voiced both regret and joy that he is now able to have fun with his grandkids in a way that he could never enjoy his own kids due to his PTSD symptoms as a young adult.

> *Thomas withdrew from his family, and Christine pointed*
> *out that he needs to get help. This "wake-up call" has*
> *provided Thomas with the motivation to seek treatment*
> *for PTSD and will give him the chance to reopen those*
> *emotional connections to his wife and daughters as his*
> *PTSD symptoms improve and his drinking is reduced.*

PTSD also impacts work. As you can imagine, when images of trauma pop into your head, it is hard to maintain concentration. If you need to concentrate in your work, this can impact your speed of performance, your ability to learn new information, or even your general ability to focus on conversations. When a survivor is also irritable and tired, this makes work even more difficult. Extreme sleep deprivation can result in dangerous work errors for people in manufacturing or other industries where focus is especially important. And for those people with PTSD who are still in the military or who are engaged in other professions (such as first responders) that involve regular exposure to threatening conditions, this can place them at increased risk of developing problems with each additional trauma exposure, if those earlier traumas are not addressed. Police officers often report having a higher sense of danger than a specific circumstance warrants based on past incidents that involved them having to use deadly force or where their fellow officers were hurt or killed.

> *For Cynthia, her school work suffered as she could not maintain focus to complete the assignments. She avoided attending classes as she feared her rapist would be there and watching her. When she tried to study, the images from her assault came crashing in, along with the smell of his sweat and the sound of his gruff voice telling her that he would come back and kill her if she told anyone. Cynthia received incompletes for most of her classes, and she barely passed those classes she did complete. She felt totally derailed and unable to get her feet back under her. She did not know what to do next as she spoke to her counselor about withdrawing from school.*

How is PTSD diagnosed? Is there a blood test for it?

PTSD is diagnosed through clinical interview with a mental health professional. This may be done by a psychologist, psychiatric nurse, social worker, or psychiatrist. Nowadays, mental health care is moving to primary care, and many primary care providers can diagnose common mental health conditions, such as PTSD. Assessment to identify a specific traumatic event will typically start the process. A "target trauma" is the life-threatening event that is stuck and haunting the person most over the recent past (often focus on the past 2 to 4 weeks). Once a specific event is identified, then examination of the symptoms of PTSD will occur, including all 20 symptoms included in the four clusters in the DSM-5. As discussed near the start of this chapter, the clusters of PTSD include intrusion, avoidance, negative alterations in cognition and mood, and alterations in arousal and reactivity. Examination of all four clusters in relationship to a specific target trauma is needed to accurately make the PTSD diagnosis.

To aid in assessment and improve reliability and accuracy of the diagnosis, the best way to test for PTSD is by the healthcare provider using a structured clinical interview for PTSD. There are a number of these, with the most widely used being the Clinician-Administered PTSD Scale for DSM-5 (CAPS-5)[1] and the PTSD Symptom Scale Interview for DSM-5 (PSSI-5). In addition, there are questionnaires that the survivor herself can fill out, with the most common called the PTSD Checklist for DSM-5 (PCL-5)[2] and the Posttraumatic Diagnostic Scale for DSM-5 (PDS-5).

While generally not yet in popular use, biological tests to evaluate how to help trauma survivors are beginning to provide information for patient care. Some clinics test the survivor's heart rate, skin conductance (sweating), and breathing to determine who is most likely to respond more quickly or more slowly to psychotherapy, and this feedback can help to create ways to assist those individuals who may be slower to respond to psychotherapy. As research continues to clarify how treatment works and who it works for, additional testing is likely to occur to help us decide which is the right treatment for each person.

How common is PTSD?

Research in the United States shows that about 4 percent of American adults have had PTSD in the past year and about 7 percent have had it over their lifetime. Women are about twice as likely as men to develop PTSD. It is not clear why this is the case, and research is looking into this. But the rates of exposure to the types of trauma that puts survivors at the highest risk of developing PTSD (such as sexual assault) contributes to this gender difference. Rates for developing PTSD among certain populations are much higher than for the general population, including rates among those with alcohol or substance abuse issues. Rates also tend to be higher in younger adults than older adults. Rates among military populations range between 6 and 8 percent.

PTSD is not a common disorder, but when it occurs, it can wreck the lives of trauma survivors and their families. As you will see in the next chapter, there are several options for effective treatment, including medication and psychotherapy. These treatments can lead to a lessening of PTSD symptoms or can even lead to getting over the disorder altogether.

What online tools are available for people who want to learn more about trauma survivors and PTSD?

While many sites on the Internet are presented as though they have a magic cure for PTSD, survivors should be cautious and do their best to make sure that the source of information is legitimate. Many people may be well intentioned but not have a true understanding of the disorder and the most effective treatments. Others are simply out to make money off of people who are suffering. The following sites are all from sources approved by well-respected experts in PTSD:

The National Association for the Mentally Ill (NAMI; https://www.nami.org/Learn-More/Mental-Health-Conditions/Posttraumatic-Stress-Disorder/Support) has many online resources to connect someone suffering with PTSD or their family to information, crisis intervention, and clinical treatment resources.

Similarly, the National Institute of Mental Health (https://www.helpguide.org/articles/ptsd-trauma/ptsd-symptoms-self-help-treatment.htm/) has information and resources for those suffering with PTSD from all types of trauma.

One online resource that is very helpful for trauma survivors and their families is AboutFace (https://www.ptsd.va.gov/apps/aboutface/). This online site developed by the National Center for PTSD in the Department of Veterans Affairs presents the stories of Veterans who have survived trauma and then engaged in PTSD treatment. The stories are presented as videos of the Veterans themselves and their family members. In these videos, they talk about the specifics of their PTSD and their treatment so that others can get familiar with what to expect and how treatment works. While the site is focused on military trauma, the stories are wide-ranging with hundreds of Veterans represented and discussing combat, military sexual trauma, and other traumas. While some of the content can be upsetting to hear, the stories of seeking care and getting help are encouraging and enlightening for those suffering with PTSD, their families, and the community at large. Since this is a VA-developed resource, the stories are focused on Veterans, but many civilian trauma survivors have voiced similar experiences and stories. For instance, sexual trauma survivors tell us they can relate to the stories of military sexual trauma survivors who have been raped.

Similarly, the Make the Connection website (https://maketheconnection.net/conditions/ptsd) has the stories of many Veterans and service members connecting to care for PTSD related to military and non-military traumas and other mental health issues.

Another resource developed for military service members and Veterans is *Afterdeployment.org* (https://www.afterdeployment.org/). This site offers education as well as some focused online treatment resources for military service members and their families following deployment. As with AboutFace, some of these resources for PTSD are also relevant to nonmilitary trauma survivors.

In addition to the online information about PTSD and PTSD treatment, there are some specific apps that are useful for people with PTSD and their families. Many of these apps were developed by the VA and the Department of Defense but were created for use by people who have survived many different types of trauma, not just military-related. PTSD Coach (https://mobile.va.gov/app/ptsd-coach) is an app that is designed for coping with the symptoms of PTSD. It is not a treatment, but many people suffering with PTSD have found it helpful to use prior to treatment or even after treatment to maintain gains and explore new ways to cope with anxiety and stress as well as PTSD.

The National Center for PTSD website (https://www.ptsd. va.gov/) includes many resources for survivors and their family and friends to learn about deployment, trauma, PTSD, and its treatment. The resources range from written materials on the latest research findings about the development and treatment of PTSD to online videos and whiteboard videos about how treatment works or how to access care. While these often focus on Veterans and military, other types of trauma such as sexual assault and child abuse are also represented.

All of these resources are provided as a way to get you started learning about PTSD, but if you are a survivor and decide it is time to seek treatment, connecting with a licensed mental health provider with specific training in evidence-based treatments for PTSD is warranted. We discuss treatment options for PTSD in Chapter 4 of this volume.

Notes

1. Weathers, F. W., Blake, D. D., Schnurr, P. P., Kaloupek, D. G., Marx, B. P., & Keane, T. M. (2013). The Clinician-Administered PTSD Scale for DSM-5 (CAPS-5). *National Center for PTSD*. Retrieved from www.ptsd.va.gov
2. Blevins, C. A., Weathers, F. W., Davis, M. T., Witte, T. K., & Domino, J. L. (2015). The Posttraumatic Stress Disorder Checklist for DSM-5 (PCL-5): Development and initial psychometric evaluation. *Journal of Traumatic Stress, 28*(6), 489–498. doi:10.1002/jts.22059

4

WHAT ARE THE TREATMENTS FOR PTSD?

In Chapter 3 of this book, we described what it's like to live with PTSD. The bad news is it stinks to have PTSD, as it disrupts people's lives, health, and relationships. And as hard as it is to live with PTSD, it is also hard to live with someone with PTSD. The good news is that we have several effective treatments for PTSD, so even if the first treatment doesn't work, there are other effective treatments that can be tried.

What kinds of people treat PTSD? How do I know if they are good?

In general, treatments for PTSD can be divided into psychotherapy and medication. Psychotherapy, sometimes known as "talk therapy" is usually done one on one with a therapist and the person suffering from PTSD. Therapists must be providers licensed by the state in which they practice.

- Psychologists, one type of provider, typically have a PhD in clinical psychology but may have a PsyD and are not licensed to prescribe medication.
- In most states, social workers can also be licensed to deliver therapy. Social workers typically have a master's degree in social work (e.g., MSW).

- Psychiatrists are medical doctors (MDs). They may prescribe medications and may also provide therapy.
- In some states, physician assistants (PAs) and clinical nurse specialists (CNSs) may also prescribe medications supervised by a physician.

You can look online at your secretary of state website and make sure your provider is licensed. It is fine to ask a prospective provider questions about their experience treating PTSD and what kinds of treatments they use. Most people want to find a provider covered by their insurance plan, but it is even more important to find a provider who is experienced with effective treatments for PTSD. Most of the effective treatments that we describe for PTSD do not require that many sessions, so even if the best provider is out of network, it may be a good short-term investment for long-term gain.

What kinds of therapies help PTSD?

The types of therapy that have been shown to be helpful for PTSD are known as "trauma-focused therapies." They were specifically designed or adapted for PTSD. Some therapies are more generic, but trauma-focused therapy looks at specific thoughts and habits that have become a problem since the trauma. Most of these are forms of cognitive behavior therapy (CBT). CBT

- tends to be very problem-focused (rather than focusing on the unconscious),
- is usually short-term (usually weeks rather than months),
- commonly has a skills-based focus (the therapist teaches skills in session), and
- usually involves assigning homework to practice the skills taught in the session.

CBT is very effective at treating problems involving anxiety and depression. For most anxiety and depressive problems, CBT would be recommended to try before trying medication if the person is new to treatment. Once people learn the CBT skills in therapy, they are told to continue practicing these skills even after therapy ends. When they do continue to practice the skills, there is very little relapse. If a new stressful situation, like the loss of a relationship or job, or another trauma occurs, sometimes symptoms can increase. However, if the trauma survivor goes back to the skills that worked to treat PTSD, such increases tend to be temporary. The trauma-focused therapies that have been shown to be consistently effective in treating PTSD include prolonged exposure[1] (PE) and other types of exposure therapy, cognitive therapy, cognitive processing therapy[2] (CPT), and eye movement desensitization and reprocessing[3] (EMDR).

What is prolonged exposure (PE)?

One of the treatments that has been studied the most for PTSD is PE. In exposure therapy, people are helped to confront situations that scare them—but that are realistically safe—in a therapeutic manner to lessen their fear, anxiety, and distress. A classic example of exposure is the advice to a rider to "get back on the horse" after being thrown off. In doing so, the rider overcomes her fear of being thrown again, which prevents the fear from growing. As we mentioned in an earlier chapter, most PTSD therapists and researchers think that avoidance is part of what keeps PTSD symptoms going. Therefore, PE is aimed at helping the person confront the memory of the traumatic experience and reminders of the event, but in a safe way, so that their distress decreases and the person learns that he can handle it and that it is not 100 percent dangerous. Trauma survivors, like Cynthia and Thomas, need to learn that the world is not as dangerous as they perceive it to be or that their bodies are telling them it is. In addition, they need to learn that they can handle the distress linked to the memory/reminders and that their distress will get better if they let themselves revisit the memory/reminders, including the emotions they were feeling during that time. Finally, they learn that what they fear will not happen: No one gets hurt. The distress does increase, but it doesn't stay up forever and eventually comes back down even while they are still confronting what scares them. The emotional pain is not unbearable. They are able to emerge on the other side of it. As they *approach* the memory and reminders instead of *avoiding* them, they can reclaim their lives from PTSD. If their lives have become narrow from avoidance, many people with PTSD also need to learn to become more active and socially engaged if they have become isolated. PE helps survivors do this.

PE is a way to help trauma survivors emotionally process their traumatic experiences. Doing this reduces PTSD and other trauma-related problems. PE includes the following key components:

- Education about common reactions to trauma, what maintains trauma-related symptoms, and how PE reduces PTSD symptoms;
- Repeated real-life exposure (called "in vivo" exposure) to situations, people, or objects that are objectively safe or low risk but that the person is avoiding because these situations are trauma-related and cause emotional distress, such as anxiety, shame, or guilt; and
- Repeated "imaginal exposure" to the trauma memories (that is, revisiting and recounting aloud the trauma memory in a person's imagination) followed by talking about the event, emotions, and thoughts that the person had during the trauma. This is done through discussion of the experience of recounting the trauma memories.

In vivo and imaginal exposures are the core of the PE treatment. These techniques were selected because there is a great deal of evidence showing that they effectively reduce anxiety and distress in people who suffer from anxiety disorders, such as specific phobias, panic disorder, social anxiety disorder, and obsessive-compulsive disorder. Thirty years of research have shown that PE is effective in reducing PTSD and other trauma-related problems such as depression, general anxiety, guilt, substance use, and anger. Obviously, there are no guarantees about how any one person will respond, but this program has helped tens of thousands of people around the world.

The aim of in vivo and imaginal exposure is to help trauma survivors emotionally process the traumatic events by helping them face the memories of their trauma and the situations that are associated with these memories. *This is a powerful way to learn that the memories of the trauma and the situations or activities that are associated with these memories are not the same as the trauma itself.* Survivors will learn that they can safely think about their trauma and experience the trauma reminders. The anxiety and distress that they feel at first will go down over time, and they begin to feel confident that they can tolerate this anxiety. It is through this process of learning that they can handle distress and previously feared memories and situations that they reclaim their lives from PTSD.

By doing the things that scare us, including confronting trauma memories and reminders, trauma survivors learn that they can tolerate these situations and that nothing bad happens. They learn that their distress will go down even while confronting what they have been avoiding. They learn that they don't go crazy or lose control. Imaginal and in vivo exposure exercises help PTSD sufferers tell the difference between the traumatic event and other similar—but nondangerous—events. Understanding this difference allows survivors to see the trauma as a specific event occurring in space and time, which helps them get over feelings and thoughts that the world is entirely dangerous and they are completely incompetent to deal with it.

People with PTSD often say that thinking about the traumatic event makes it feel as if the event is happening all over again, which is partly why they avoid thinking about it. Repeated imaginal exposure to the trauma memory helps people tell the difference between the past and present. It helps them realize that although remembering the trauma can be emotionally upsetting, the trauma is not happening again, and therefore *thinking about the event* is not dangerous. Repeated imaginal exposure also helps people think differently about what happened to them. For example, someone who feels guilty about not having done more to resist an attacker may soon realize that she did resist as much as she could have or that the assault might have been even worse if she had resisted more. All of these changes reduce PTSD symptoms and bring about a sense of mastery and competence.

PE typically consists of 8 to 15 weekly or twice-weekly treatment sessions that are each generally 90 minutes long, working one on one with a therapist. In the first three sessions, the therapist

- gathers information about the traumatic experience and the person's reaction,
- explains how the treatment works,
- discusses imaginal exposure and in vivo exposure in more detail,
- plans the treatment by creating a list of avoided situations that will be used for exposure, and
- makes sure the PTSD sufferer fully understands the therapy.

Starting in session 2, the therapist will help the survivor confront situations in real life (in vivo exposure) that the survivor has been avoiding because these situations remind the survivor of the trauma—but such situations are realistically safe. For example, for motor vehicle crash survivors, in vivo exposure will include driving and driving near where the crash occurred. Usually, this is assigned as homework.

Imaginal exposure to the memory of the traumatic experience (i.e., revisiting the memory) is begun in session 3. The therapist will guide the PTSD sufferer to close his or her eyes and recount the trauma memory in the present tense out loud, as if it is happening now. Together they go through this memory several times per session for a total of about 45 minutes. The therapist will record this recounting for the survivor to listen to for homework between sessions. In each session of imaginal exposure, the therapist will encourage the survivor to dig a little deeper and recount more details, not leaving anything out. A patient workbook for PE describes the sessions and treatment in more detail.[4]

Even though standard practice is for the survivor to see the therapist once or twice a week, there are a few programs in the United States and Europe that offer PE as an intensive outpatient program in which sufferers go to the clinic all day, every day, for 2 weeks.[5]

Why can't trauma survivors just expose themselves? Why do they need to do it with a therapist?

Trauma survivors with PTSD have had an interruption in the natural recovery process. As we discussed previously, most people immediately following a trauma have symptoms that we would later call PTSD (intrusive images of the trauma, problems sleeping, hypervigilance, etc.). Many people are able to do the things they have to do in life and approach relatively safe but trauma-related people, places, and situations. Over time, things get easier for these people, as they continue to approach these situations and engage in their lives. This is natural recovery. However, those trauma survivors who avoid rather than approach people, places, and things because these are associated with the trauma or make them feel uncomfortable, continue to experience anxiety, which may even increase in intensity. In addition, avoided items often increase over time. By the time a survivor has PTSD, that fear and anxiety can be quite intense and entrenched and their lives have become very narrow. Survivors with PTSD will sometimes ask us how this is different from what they are currently doing, as they are getting triggered maybe hundreds of times each day. We explain that in PE, we are going to do things differently. To use an analogy of reading a book, before treatment, they may open the book, get triggered, then slam it shut. This may happen many times per day. In PE, we will start reading that book from the beginning and read every word over and over again to the end until we can make some sense out of it and read it with less distress. It is part of the story of their lives and needs to be incorporated into a way they can live with.

If survivors want to start approaching trauma-related situations again, that is a great sign that they can benefit from treatment. Getting started with exposures on their own can be helpful if they approach it in the way that in vivo exposures are done in PE. The problem is that most survivors with PTSD will tend to avoid—in small and large ways—as exposures can be difficult. For example, any time an exposure is done where survivors are engaging in safety behaviors, or approaching the situation without clearly thinking through the goal of the exposure, or leaving the exposure when very distressed, there is high potential for the exposure to not have the best outcome. Specifically, survivors may become even more convinced that the situation is dangerous if they try to approach it and it does not go as they may have thought it would go in their head. For exposure to be therapeutic, it needs to be

1. planned to be very clear what is the goal of the exposure (what is being approached and why);

2. a long enough duration that the survivor experiences an increase and reduction in anxiety and learns that their distress will decrease while still in the situation and that the situation is not inherently as dangerous as it might feel;

3. repeated often enough to show gains over time and generalization, that is, to get easier over time and show benefits in other situations; and

4. reviewed and discussed as far as what the survivor learned from the given exposure (harder or easier than expected, how does this impact their views of their self and the world, etc.).

Because avoidance is so strong in PTSD, once a survivor has developed PTSD, it is unlikely that they will fully approach the exposure without support and planning from someone who does not have PTSD, such as a therapist. It is the job of the PTSD therapist to work to notice and quickly address active and passive avoidance to ensure that the survivor gets the most out of each exposure in which they engage. This includes setting up the difficulty so that it is not so hard that the survivor will not succeed and is not so easy that they do not have a sense of accomplishment. A therapist will also watch for safety behaviors that may be hidden, such as carrying a pill bottle with their anxiety meds in their pocket as a comfort or only going with another person or at a certain time of day. We tell people undergoing exposure therapy that we will push them out of their comfort zones, but not out of their safety zones.

What about virtual reality?

Virtual reality exposure (VRE) therapy uses computer technology to create a 3D immersive world that the user can interact with. Users usually wear a head-mounted display, which is like a helmet, with a little television screen in front of each eye, earphones, and a position tracker. As the wearer moves her head, the position tracker picks up the movement and changes the view inside the head mounted display in real time. Many applications use a hand held sensor or joystick to help maneuver in the virtual environment.

In VRE, the therapist displays what the person is describing and changes it to match what the person says. It is almost exactly like PE as previously described except that the person's eyes are open so they can see the virtual environment. Most of the virtual environments used for PTSD are for war Veterans, although they also depict motor vehicle crashes, terrorist attacks, and natural disasters.

If we wanted to use VRE for Thomas, we would use a virtual Humvee. We could place him in the driver's seat and let him drive the vehicle down a desert highway with his comrades in the seats beside and behind him. We would explode the improvised explosive device as he is describing it exploding in his imaginal exposure and fill the vehicle with smoke and allow him to exit the vehicle when he describes doing that. We can repeat this as many times as Thomas needs.

What is cognitive therapy?

Cognitive therapy helps the PTSD sufferer examine how the traumatic experience has changed the way they think and correct those thoughts where they are not accurate or not helpful. Following a traumatic event, some people think they can never be safe again and that there is danger lurking around every corner. They may feel guilty about what happened during the event or what they did to survive. If others didn't survive, they may experience what we call "survivor's guilt." They may feel dirty or bad or worthless. Often, it is hard to trust others. In cognitive therapy, the therapist helps the trauma survivor identify these unhelpful and inaccurate thoughts. Together they examine how accurate these thoughts are and then replace them with more helpful and more accurate thoughts. Homework usually involves practicing identifying and challenging these unhelpful thoughts by writing them down.

Cognitive therapy typically lasts about 8 to 12 sessions and is usually done weekly with an individual therapist.

What is cognitive processing therapy (CPT)?

CPT is a specific form of trauma-focused cognitive therapy based on questioning the assumptions and beliefs arising as a result of traumatic events. CPT involves identifying, challenging, and replacing unhelpful and distorted thoughts and beliefs about oneself and the traumatic experience with more helpful thoughts. These unhelpful thoughts about the trauma and its impact on the survivor are called *stuck points* and much of CPT focuses on these thoughts. Session 1 of CPT begins with general education about PTSD and discussion with the patient about her experience of trauma and PTSD and the general overview and rationale for the protocol. This discussion includes stuck points and how they contribute to avoidance and PTSD following trauma as well as different ways to adapt thinking after a traumatic event so that it doesn't interfere with functioning, including changing memories to fit beliefs and not over applying what was learned from a trauma context to other contexts. The session ends with directing the survivor to complete her first impact statement about how the trauma has impacted her. This impact statement will form the basis for much of the work to come and provides the first information to identify stuck points. Session 2 begins with review of the impact statement and moves on to covering how events, thoughts, and feelings are related. Once this concept is covered, the survivor is instructed in how to complete thought monitoring sheets (called ABC sheets) as a tool to look for her own unhelpful thoughts and patterns of thinking that maintain PTSD. Session 3 then starts the process of cognitive restructuring through thought challenging using the ABC sheets.

There are several versions of CPT, and some involve writing a trauma narrative (story of what happened) as homework in sessions 3 and 4 and reading it in sessions 4 and 5 with the therapist. The narratives, or the ABC sheets if the trauma narrative is not used, provide the basis to identify stuck points that usually center around the themes of safety, trust, power/control, esteem, and intimacy. The remainder of sessions focus on more in-depth cognitive challenge of these stuck points, using thought challenge sheets, which help the survivor work through a stuck point thought and then identify an alternate thought that will be more helpful. Finally, the last sessions focus on each of the five previously noted themes. CPT usually takes about 12 sessions and can be done one on one or in a group.

Ensuring that survivors are completing their thought monitoring and challenge forms in real time is very important for CPT. Survivors who have a hard time writing can try typing the forms out or even recording responses to the questions from the sheet. The key is beginning to notice the patterns of thoughts and working to replace the stuck points with more helpful alternate thoughts.

What is eye movement desensitization and reprocessing (EMDR)?

In EMDR, the therapist asks the PTSD sufferer to bring up a mental picture that represents the worst moment in the traumatic event. The survivor and the therapist identify words that go with that picture. These are not necessarily words that were said at the time of the trauma, but rather words that have endured such as, "I'm not safe." The therapist then asks the survivor to identify what emotion they are feeling when they get that picture and remember those words and where in their body they are feeling the emotion. While they have this picture in their mind's eye, rehearsing the words, and focusing on the feeling in their body, the therapist typically holds up two fingers and moves them from side to side in front of the survivor's eyes. The survivor is asked to track the therapist's fingers moving back and forth producing a back and forth eye movement. Between EMDR tasks, the therapist checks in with the survivor to see if anything about the picture, the words, or the feelings has changed and then helps the survivor focus for the next set of eye movements. Once the distress associated with the memory decreases, the survivor and the therapist are able to explore the meaning associated with the event and work on new ways to think about it. EMDR is given one on one by a therapist, usually once a week, for approximately 4 to 12 sessions.

EMDR works similarly to PE in that the survivor is asked to focus on many aspects of the traumatic experience—the picture, the words, the emotions—and process what this all means repeatedly until the distress decreases and thoughts about the event change. To some survivors, the back and forth eye movements can seem strange at first. Some EMDR providers and researchers think that the back and forth eye movements help to process emotional material, like in rapid eye movement (REM) sleep when we are dreaming. Other providers and researchers think that the back and forth eye movements are a distraction from our usual avoidance strategies and therefore allow the distressing material to be processed.

During a session or course of EMDR, sometimes the picture changes, sometimes the words change, sometimes the feelings change. Typically, we start with the worst—the worst memory that brings up the most unpleasant feelings. The first session usually focuses on this worst memory. The therapist asks the survivor to get the scene in her mind's eye, focus on the words and the feelings, while following with her eyes the therapist's fingers moving back and forth approximately a foot in front of the patient's face. After a "set" of eye movements, the therapist instructs the survivor to "blank it out" and take a deep breath. Then the therapist asks the survivor to bring back up the picture, the words, and the feelings and "tell me what you get." It is like a dance between the survivor and therapist. When the survivor recounts what comes up, the therapist helps direct what the survivor should focus on during the next set of eye movements. In this back and forth way, the survivor usually moves through what happened in the traumatic memory, what it brings up for him or her, and other experiences it is related to, and gets to a place that feels better and less intrusive. Sometimes survivors report that the scene fades or feels more distant. Often times survivors report a new perspective on the traumatic event such as, "I made it. He can't hurt me anymore," or "It's in the past." Usually the survivor reports that the feelings associated with the memory are less intense and intrusive.

What does evidence-based care mean?

Evidence-based care means (a) that the treatments have been objectively evaluated and shown in studies to work and (b) that providers are using these treatments that have been shown in studies to work in their care of patients. If there are no treatments that have been shown to work, or if the treatments that have been shown to work on others are not helpful for a particular person, evidence-based care also means (c) gathering objective evidence on the treatment provided to be able to look at whether it's working or not. Therapists using their clinical judgment about what to do and feeling that it was helpful is not evidence-based care. We recommend evidence-based care. An example not related to PTSD might help explain what we mean if a specific antibiotic has been shown to be helpful (a), the doctor should use that medication when a patient with that infection comes to her (b). If that medication doesn't help that patient, however, the doctor should try another antibiotic and evaluate it objectively (c) by gathering evidence as to whether it was helpful or not. By doing this systematically, providers are giving their patients the best chance to receive an effective treatment for that condition.

What about other treatments?

There are many well-meaning therapists delivering treatments that they hope will be helpful for people with PTSD. However, if these treatments have not been evaluated in research studies, it is difficult to know how helpful they are and for whom. For the best results, we encourage people suffering with PTSD to work with providers trained in these evidence-based treatments for the best chance of success.

What tools or resources are available for people working through PTSD treatment?

Many apps are now available for mental health care and are targeted at PTSD, depression, and other issues that trauma survivors may confront. However, many of these apps have not been evaluated for how helpful they are. In considering whether to use an app, a trauma survivor should first think about what their goal is in using it. Is this app intended to help them feel better temporarily (in the moment), or are they expecting this to address the PTSD or depression as a treatment? If the goal is to treat or get rid of PTSD, then discussion with a treatment provider about the app and its usefulness may be a good idea.

Since mental health expertise is not a requirement to design and market an app, the public should be cautious when using such apps and look for evidence that the app is developed by people with expertise in mental health care and PTSD. Some apps, developed by non-PTSD experts, actually encourage avoidance, which is more likely to maintain PTSD over time or even lead to more problems. For example, some well-intentioned, although unhelpful, apps inform trauma survivors that their heart rate is increasing and tell them to stop what they're doing. For a trauma survivor with PTSD, this increase may be happening due to trauma triggers or to normal alterations in heart rate that all people have. However, some of these apps then suggest that the survivor stop what they are doing and lower their heart rate through a breathing exercise. While this may *seem* helpful, as the survivor is reducing what the app registers as anxiety, it may be that the survivor is walking fast (not even related to trauma) or is seeing a trigger that increases heart rate but is not dangerous. To stop what they are doing to reduce their heart rate may negatively impact their ability to accomplish what they need to do in life and will increase awareness of every possible obstacle or trigger in the environment. It is also encouraging them to avoid, the opposite of what we think a trauma survivor should be doing.

As part of effective therapy for PTSD, we usually advise trauma survivors to encounter triggers that aren't dangerous and stay in the situations long enough for their distress to decrease to learn that the situation isn't dangerous and their bodies will calm down even while still confronting the trigger. This is exactly the opposite of what some of the apps instruct. Therefore, we recommend getting advice from someone who is knowledgeable about PTSD before using any app or self-help program.

If a survivor is functioning relatively well and just needs a little boost or way to encourage more positive coping, there are lots of options for apps that can assist (e.g., daily meditation apps and exercise motivation apps). If, however, a survivor is really distressed (experiencing problems in their functioning and family functioning and likely suffering with PTSD), then seeking the help of a mental health professional to get them going on the right path may be a better option.

What online tools or apps are available for people in treatment for PTSD?

Several apps for use while engaging in evidence-based interventions for PTSD and related problems have been developed by the Department of Veterans Affairs (VA). Two of the most relevant to PTSD are PE Coach and CPT Coach. The apps are intended to ease completion of required activities in the therapy. They also include prerecorded versions of much of the psychoeducation material for the trauma survivor with PTSD to review or reinforce the messages in session. They are free to download and use.

PE Coach (https://mobile.va.gov/app/pe-coach-2) is an app that is intended for use while working with a therapist in PE therapy. This app can assist with secure recording of the trauma memory that is part of this treatment as well as planning for practice exercises and recording of distress ratings as the trauma survivor works through the exposures in PE to take their life back from PTSD.

CPT Coach (https://mobile.va.gov/app/cpt-coach) is an app intended for use while working with a therapist in CPT. The app provides many of the forms for cognitive restructuring and psychoeducational materials explaining why the treatment works. Both apps are intended to be used while in treatment with a PE or CPT provider and not as self-help treatments. Several other apps for use in therapy are also available through the VA app site (https://mobile.va.gov/appstore).

Another app, the CBT-I Coach (https://mobile.va.gov/app/cbt-i-coach), may be useful for those trauma survivors suffering from primary insomnia who may be working through CBT for insomnia (CBT-I) with a mental health professional. This app provides a convenient way to record sleep and sleep quality as well as tools to assist with sleep restriction and psychoeducation on sleep hygiene.

Are there medications for PTSD?

Selective serotonin reuptake inhibitor (SSRIs)

Sertraline (Zoloft) and paroxetine (Paxil) are the only medications approved by the U.S. Food and Drug Administration for use in treating PTSD. These drugs belong in the class of medications called selective serotonin reuptake inhibitors (SSRIs). It is common for people already taking either of these drugs or other appropriate medication for PTSD and/or depression to enter therapy. If a survivor is already taking these medications and still suffers from PTSD, he can stay on the medication and go through a trauma-focused therapy because we have not found the medication to interfere with this treatment. We would suggest in most cases that the sufferer maintains the same medication at the same dose over the course of therapy to reduce the chance that changes in medication or dosage interfere with the therapy. Specifically, PTSD symptoms in the first few weeks of therapy may get worse. This does not mean that things won't go well in therapy and is not a reason to increase the medication. In addition, recent research suggests that starting medication and psychotherapy at the same time does not lead to greater benefit. We suggest starting either with psychotherapy or medication—based on patient and provider discussion of options—and then only adding the other one based on any remaining symptoms after a full course of the therapy or medication.

What about MDMA?

3,4-methylenedioxy-methamphetamine (MDMA) is a drug very different from other medications for PTSD. It is known as a psychedelic and is typically characterized by 2 to 6 hours of subjective feelings of well-being, sociability, and positive mood. It has been known as a party drug, often referred to as "ecstasy" or "molly." However, there is no telling what has been mixed with MDMA when people take it on the street. The studies with PTSD have all been with pharmaceutical grade MDMA that is tested and controlled. Given its potential to reduce fear responding, enhance fear extinction, and increase prosocial emotional states, MDMA has been proposed as a candidate for assisting psychological therapies in traumatized people. The effects of MDMA-assisted psychotherapy have been evaluated in several studies and have been very promising. Studies are being conducted across the United States and in other countries testing the combination of MDMA and psychotherapy for PTSD. We will soon test the combination of MDMA and PE for people who haven't responded to other treatments for PTSD. In the United States, the Food and Drug Administration has granted Breakthrough Therapy Designation for MDMA-assisted psychotherapy. We do not recommend using MDMA alone as a way to help PTSD or other problems. As we said, (a) getting MDMA on the streets can be dangerous, and (b) the therapeutic effects are thought to be due to the combination of MDMA and therapist-led psychotherapy for PTSD.

What about yoga and other wellness activities?

Yoga is not a treatment for PTSD, but it is a great practice for a healthy life and positive coping. Many of the intensive PE programs offer yoga as a wellness exercise. Any practice that promotes a healthy lifestyle and positive coping are recommended including yoga, exercise, sleep hygiene (good sleep habits), healthy diet, and good communication skills with family.

What is sleep hygiene, and why is it important?

Sleep hygiene refers to good sleep habits. Problems with sleep are common following trauma, and this is normal. In fact, many people will have problems falling or staying asleep after experiencing a life-threatening event. What a trauma survivor does in response to sleep problems can have a significant impact on whether these problems are temporary and get better with time or are maintained over time.

For some trauma survivors, insomnia can be an ongoing issue. If survivors react to sleep problems with unhelpful thoughts, such as "I will never sleep well again" or "I have to get to sleep tonight, or I won't be able to function tomorrow," they are more likely to have worsening insomnia over time. In addition to unhelpful thoughts and insomnia, if trauma survivors develop unhelpful sleep habits and poor sleep hygiene, they are also more likely to have problems over time. The suggestions that follow for sleep hygiene can be helpful right after trauma as well as for those who develop PTSD and have continued sleep problems.

Sleep hygiene is always important. For trauma survivors who develop PTSD over time, sleep hygiene can be even more important. PTSD disrupts sleep in many people so good sleep hygiene becomes even more important. Some of the rules of good sleep hygiene include the following:

- *Reduce stimulants late in the day, including caffeine and sugar.* Most people can wait to stop consuming stimulants (like drinking caffeinated coffee or eating chocolate) until after dinner and that is fine to not interfere with sleep, but for some people who are sensitive to caffeine or sugar or chocolate, stopping consumption at lunchtime may make it easier to fall asleep.
- *Avoid alcohol close to bedtime.* Even though it may make you feel drowsy, alcohol actually interferes with good sleep. With alcohol, the typical guide is to stop drinking about 2 hours before going to sleep.
- *Standardize life routines (sleep–wake, meals, exercise).* We suggest going to sleep and waking up at the same time every day, including weekends. When your body is used to a pattern of sleep and wake, it is more able to maintain the cycle when other things vary (such as life stress).
- *Avoid strenuous physical activity close to bedtime.* Exercise is great, but not too close to bedtime. Experts suggest stopping strenuous exercise at least an hour before going to sleep.
- *Never look at the clock when you are trying to sleep.* Turn the clock away from you to avoid looking at the time. Looking at the clock wakes you up more, which you do not want to do when you are trying to sleep. To see the

time, you may have to physically change positions and raise your head, and then light comes in at a time when it is supposed to be dark. You may then have thoughts about what time it is, and your body can react to those thoughts and wake you up even more. There is never a good time for it to be when you are trying to sleep and are not asleep. If it is early in the night when you look at the clock, this might cause stress worrying it will be a bad night. If it is early in the morning, it might cause stress worrying that you won't get back to sleep and you will be tired the next day. It is important to remember that we have all had less than restful sleep, and we do actually function fine the next day. It is not a catastrophe.

- *Go to bed when sleepy.* Don't lie down until you feel like you will sleep soon after your head hits the pillow. Being tired and sleepy are not the same thing. When you are sleepy, don't keep doing something else; stop that activity and go to sleep.
- *Use the bed only for sleep (and sex).* We don't want the bed associated with not sleeping, so only get in bed to sleep or have sex. It is not a spot to read or watch television routinely.
- *Get out of bed if you're not sleeping and only return when sleepy.* If you are not asleep in the amount of time it should take you to get to sleep, get out of bed and do something else. Do not do something activating or stimulating—do something boring. Do not get on the computer or use any screen.
- *No screen time 1 hour before bed.* Research has shown that looking at computer or tablet or phone screens close to bedtime interferes with sleep.
- *Set an alarm and wake up at the same time every day.* Set the alarm for the time you really need to wake up. Then when it goes off, get out of bed. **Do not hit the snooze button**. Hitting the snooze button may feel luxurious, but it is not good-quality sleep and therefore is wasting

time. Some people tell us they feel more groggy after hitting the snooze button.

- *Avoid naps.* In the United States, our adult schedules do not include naps or *siestas*. Our schedules assume we get our sleep in one chunk at night. If we nap, we won't be ready to go to sleep when it is time, which means we might feel tired the next day, and this can become a vicious cycle.

What does "exposure" mean for a trauma survivor?

In a war zone, "exposure" means being vulnerable to threats and can be very dangerous. In public health terms, exposure means coming into contact with something that might be harmful, such as a contagious disease or contaminated area. Within the context of treatment for PTSD, however, since avoidance of trauma reminders is what helps people develop and maintain PTSD, exposure means deliberately confronting these reminders in a safe and therapeutic manner. Therefore, when we talk about treatment for PTSD, exposure is a good thing. It is still a hard thing and requires courage and bravery, but exposure is necessary to take back one's life from PTSD.

Has any organization rated treatments for PTSD?

Two different organizations published guidelines for recommendations for PTSD treatment in 2017: the American Psychological Association (APA) and the VA together with the Department of Defense (DOD). The VA and DOD worked together to produce one set of guidelines aimed at military service members and Veterans (VA/DOD Clinical Practice Guidelines). The APA guidelines apply to all trauma survivors. The conclusions of both reports are very similar.

All of the treatments that we have covered in this chapter were recommended by both guidelines. Trauma-focused CBT and PE and CPT specifically were strongly recommended by the APA guidelines and EMDR was conditionally recommended. Four medications were weakly recommended in both guidelines: sertraline (Zoloft), paroxetine (Paxil), fluoxetine (Prozac), and venlafaxine (Effexor). Anxiety-reducing medications such as benzodiazepines (e.g., Xanax, Valium, and Ativan) are not recommended for PTSD and have been shown to interfere with PE. Having people with PTSD start on both medication and psychotherapy at the same time was not recommended by either guideline because the evidence has not shown that the combination is better than just psychotherapy or medication for most people.

Does the PTSD sufferer's preference matter?

Yes! Studies have shown that if people have a preference for one treatment over another, they are likely to respond better to that treatment. Therefore, if everything is equal, choosing the treatment that sounds more appealing or acceptable to the survivor is a good idea. However, sometimes everything is not equal, and the doctor or therapist may have a specific treatment recommendation based on the problems the person is having. We do not yet have much evidence to know what specific treatment is best for a specific individual, but we are doing research to try to answer that question.

How can we tell if the treatment is working?

In evidence-based care, we measure the problems that people are having at different points in treatment. We do this to better understand what's really going on and how the person in treatment is responding to the treatment. The provider should ask the survivor standard questions to check for PTSD and probably for depression, or the patient should complete provider-supplied questionnaires at various points in treatment, certainly before and after treatment at a minimum. We like to have our patients complete the PTSD Checklist (PCL-5) and a depression measure about every other session to see how things are going. The patient and provider can review the answers together to evaluate how she is responding to treatment. The trauma-focused psychotherapies usually require at least six sessions before people start to notice any improvement and usually require at least nine sessions for a full effect. The SSRI medications don't even "kick in" for 4 weeks, so they usually require about 6 weeks to notice any improvement and usually require 12 to 24 weeks for the full effect.

Using standardized questionnaires is one way to check in and see how the person is responding to treatment. Sometimes we use devices that attach to the person's skin to look at how their body is responding—for example, how much they startle to a noise (by measuring their eye blink) or their skin conductance response (how much they are sweating on the palms of their hands).

It is important for people with PTSD to recognize the symptoms of PTSD and related problems and to notice what makes them better or what makes them worse. Sometimes people get into habits and fail to notice when something actually changes, for example, that they did *not* have a nightmare, or that they remember something about the traumatic event and it did *not* bother them as much as it used to. Sometimes it is useful for the person with PTSD to ask a close friend or family member what they notice and if they are seeing any differences. We only recommend asking a friend or family member if they know about the traumatic event, know you are in treatment, and are supportive. We don't recommend asking them if it could be a point of contention.

It is important to remember that *people in treatment are the consumers.* They should participate fully in the selection of their treatment, their providers, and assessing their responses. If they are not pleased or have concerns, they should bring these up with their provider.

What can survivors do if they feel like dropping out of treatment?

PTSD is, by its nature, a disorder of avoidance. The desire to avoid continues even after a survivor starts treatment. We can add to this avoidance that treatment for PTSD is hard work and stirs things up. Often it can feel like it's getting worse before it gets better. There is a high dropout rate from all PTSD treatments, medications, and psychotherapies that we think is due to this avoidance kicking in. We have had patients tell us that they drive to the clinic for their appointment and then just keep driving.

It is natural to feel like dropping out of treatment at some point. We tell our patients that they may think of us like going to see the dentist—nobody really looks forward to that. However, to get better, they need to stay in treatment and receive a full dose of therapy. Some survivors may feel like stopping when they start feeling a reduction in symptoms, but they still have some hard emotions or pieces of the memory that need to be addressed. Stopping treatment at this point can be especially risky since patients may later feel like the treatment did not work or the results did not last if their symptoms come back. It can be useful to think of our brains like a garden and PTSD as the weeds in the garden. As a PTSD sufferer begins treatment, if he weeds half the garden and then stops, he may get some benefit, but the weeds will come back quickly and take over again. In a similar way, if he stops approaching the trauma memory, the unhelpful thoughts and distress will remain or even get worse as he avoids. But if he weeds the whole garden and ensures that he catches any weeds as they return, then the garden will stay fruitful and healthy for the long haul. In a similar way, if a trauma survivor fully approaches the trauma memory and avoidance through treatment for the full course, the symptoms will stay reduced over time. If the survivor notices avoidance creeping in and reacts by using approaches as learned in PTSD treatment instead of avoidance, he will maintain his progress over time.

A few things may help someone stay in treatment to get the full benefit. One is for her to remember *why* she went to treatment in the first place. What has PTSD taken from her? What does she want to take back from PTSD? Survivors should be specific when trying to motivate themselves: While "taking your life back from PTSD" may work for some, for most people, it works better to get down to the specifics and say to themselves at times of difficulty exactly why they want to follow through. For some this may be "I want to go to my son's baseball games and enjoy the game," or "I want to enjoy being intimate with my partner again," or "I want to not have nightmares about the rape/combat/other trauma."

What do people who care about the survivor think? If such family members and friends can be supportive and encouraging, let them be! However, we don't recommend using a friend or family member for support during treatment if the patient's PTSD symptoms are a point of conflict or contention.

If a patient is thinking of dropping out of treatment before the treatment is over, she can ask herself to think about other times in her life when she has done something difficult and come out of it successfully. What helped her complete that?

It is also helpful to remember that treatment for PTSD doesn't take that long. We have treated people who have suffered for decades, and within several weeks they felt like they did before the traumatic event. It is hard, but it is worth it!

If a survivor feels like dropping out of treatment, the most important thing is to tell this to their therapist. The patient shouldn't worry about hurting the therapist's feelings; these professionals know this is the nature of the beast with PTSD and will be able to help problem-solve so the patient comes back. That may include making a commitment at the end of every session to come back to the next session. It is hard work, but it is pretty quick, and it is definitely worth it.

What about booster sessions?

For some survivors who complete effective PTSD treatment, a booster session may be warranted. For some survivors, this comes out of a sense that all intense feelings are related to PTSD. This is most common in patients where their culture may influence them to label strong feelings as symptoms, and they may not recognize that PTSD treatment can be effective and result in remission. While such survivors may have had a period of PTSD, this does not necessarily mean that all strong emotions for the rest of their lives is PTSD. For these survivors, a booster session focused on how to recognize a return of PTSD versus normal anxiety related to life stress (such as divorce, birth of a baby) can be extremely useful in helping them regain their sense of function and balance.

While not common, for some survivors, symptoms of PTSD may return. Most often this happens during a period of increased anxiety, due to exposure to another traumatic experience, or if they have not continued the good habits learned in therapy and fall back into patterns of avoidance. In these cases, a booster session would first focus on assessment of current functioning and resources to manage those symptoms to determine a course of care. This assessment may determine that a session focused on how to use the skills from their previous treatment again is all that is needed. Alternatively, it may suggest a short or full new treatment for a new trauma exposure is warranted. In all of these cases, if the previous treatment was effective in reducing symptoms, then providing that same treatment can be an efficient model of care while also considering how to boost maintenance of gains and specific additional interventions.

What if treatment didn't work?

Not everyone responds to every treatment for PTSD. Sometimes it's just not the right time and the survivor isn't ready, can't commit enough time, or has too much else going on in their life. Sometimes it's just not the right treatment or the right provider. Luckily, we have several "plan As." If one treatment doesn't work, it doesn't mean that another treatment won't work. If pharmacotherapy didn't help as much as hoped for, try one of the psychotherapies. If this treatment is all that a provider knows, try another therapist who can help with another treatment.

If a survivor is what we call a partial responder, meaning that some of the symptoms of PTSD are improved but not all, or not enough, there are several choices. In discussion with the therapist, they can decide why they think the treatment didn't work as well as hoped. For example, in PE, sometimes this discussion reveals the use of what we call safety behaviors. Examples of safety behaviors include the survivor's scanning and being hypervigilant during exposure or "white knuckling it" through exposures. These behaviors don't allow the survivor, and her PTSD brain and body, to learn that nothing bad happens during the exposure; the distress may go up but it will come back down, and she can tolerate the distress. If behaviors are identified that interfered with achieving a full response, it will be important to continue therapy without these behaviors. If someone didn't take their medication as prescribed—or took it now and then, only when they felt bad, or not the full prescribed dose—then they should try the full dose and take it as prescribed. The survivor should feel free to have a full and frank discussion with the provider about their response and recommendations to try to achieve a full response. There is research being conducted now on adding medications to psychotherapy or adding somatic treatments such as repeated transcranial magnetic stimulation (rTMS) prior to therapy sessions to try to boost the survivor's response.

What about anniversary reactions?

Sometimes trauma survivors notice their PTSD symptoms coming back after treatment during anniversary reactions. Very often, they don't even realize that it is an anniversary reaction. Anniversary reactions can certainly be triggered by the date (the anniversary) when the trauma occurred, but they can also be triggered by less obvious events such as the changing of seasons, air temperature, appearance of the sky, or when the survivor's child turns the same age as they themselves were at the time of the trauma. Anniversary reactions after successful treatment for PTSD do not usually require more treatment. If it is possible, we like to try to turn anniversaries into a time to take stock of how far a survivor has come since the trauma or since treatment.

Can you provide an example of what treatment would look like?

Here is an example of what treatment could look like for Cynthia, after being referred to me (one of the authors of this book) for treatment of PTSD.

First, I will assess Cynthia for PTSD, depression, substance use, and other problems that are common following rape. Once I determine that Cynthia is indeed suffering from PTSD, we could then discuss the different treatment options. Research shows that psychotherapy tends to be more effective than medication for PTSD, so I would recommend starting with psychotherapy alone. We would then discuss the two options from trauma-focused treatment that I am trained to provide: PE and EMDR. Based on my clinical judgment, I think PE would be a good choice for Cynthia because it has been shown to be extremely effective. Cynthia avoids situations that remind her of the trauma, so an exposure therapy where Cynthia can confront these situations in a safe, therapeutic manner could be very helpful for her recovery. After describing the two options, Cynthia and I decide on PE.

In my first meeting with Cynthia, I would determine what her main issues are, gathering information and aiming to make a diagnosis. I always include a trauma history, and with Cynthia it will reveal that she was in a car crash when she was 17, but she seemed to recover fully. I suspect I will also diagnose Cynthia with depression secondary to PTSD, which she may deny. I'll explain that if I'm correct, once we treat the PTSD, the depressive symptoms should improve. I'll discuss treatment choices, as previously discussed, and hopefully will gain her consent to begin PE the next session.

In the first session of PE, I will present an overview of the treatment and the procedures we will use, gather more detailed information about the rape, teach Cynthia how to do breathing exercises, and assign her homework to practice the breathing. In following sessions, I will begin by reviewing her homework and presenting the agenda for that session. In the second PE session, I'll teach Cynthia about the common reactions to rape and give her a handout. We'll discuss the rationale for exposure (why it works), emphasizing in vivo exposure, and then we will construct the in vivo exposure hierarchy list. This is a list of situations, people, places, conversations, and so on that Cynthia avoids because these things scare her or they bring up feelings and memories associated with the assault. If Cynthia denies avoiding, I will spend some time to get her to see that her "habits," like not going to school, not dating, and not going out are actually avoidances.

In session 3, I will explain all about imaginal exposure, and we will then do our first imaginal exposure of the entire rape memory. As soon as Cynthia opens her eyes from the imaginal exposure, I will ask her, "How was that for you? What did you notice?" and we will engage in emotional processing of what came out during the exposure. We will continue this process in session 4 and maybe 5. By about session 5 or 6, we will switch to looking at "hot spots" (parts of the memory that are still causing the most distress), and we will continue working on hot spots for the remainder of therapy, probably 8 to 10 sessions total. I would also use a technique called "behavioral activation" to get Cynthia to become more involved in social activities, school, and life outside her home. During the last session, we will *conduct imaginal exposure to the entire memory again, review her progress and where she still needs work, and then either end therapy or end PE and decide on other treatment goals that we would work on in another type of treatment.*

Notes

1. Foa, E. B., Hembree, E. A., Rothbaum, B. O., & Rauch, S. A. M. (2019). *Prolonged exposure therapy for PTSD (therapist guide).* New York, NY: Oxford University Press.
2. Resick, P. A., Monson, C. M., & Chard, K. M. (2016). *Cognitive processing therapy for PTSD: A comprehensive manual.* New York, NY: Guilford Press.
3. Shapiro F. (1995). *Eye movement desensitization and reprocessing: Basic principles, protocols, and procedures.* New York, NY: Guilford.
4. Rothbaum, B. O., Foa, E. B., Hembree, E. A., & Rauch, S. A. M. (2019). Reclaiming your life from a traumatic experience (patient workbook). New York, NY: Oxford University.
5. Reclaim Your Life at Emory Healthcare Veterans Program. (n.d.). *Emory Healthcare Veterans Program.* Retrieved from https://www.emoryhealthcare.org/centers-programs/veterans-program/index.html

5

HOW ARE CHILDREN IMPACTED BY TRAUMA?

Children are not just little adults. Children understand the world differently and have "rules" for the way their world is supposed to work. It can be very difficult for an adult to make sense of a traumatic event; it can be nearly impossible for a child. The impact of traumatic events on kids can be pervasive. Children are certainly resilient—just think about what terrible conditions children survive and later thrive in—but they are also still impressionable. Their nervous systems have not fully developed, and therefore trauma can have an enduring impact. Children grow up into different adults than they would have been if they had not experienced trauma. Research has shown us that kids who survive trauma can experience changes to how they view themselves and the world and can even develop changes to their biological systems. These changes then can impact how such children react to people and other stressful events as they grow up. In this chapter we will look more closely at how trauma impacts children and what we can do to reduce or prevent negative mental health effects such as posttraumatic stress disorder (PTSD).

Is trauma common in children?

While we all wish that we could keep children safe from trauma, children are exposed to all the same types of traumatic events that we have described in the previous chapters for adults. Sadly, following a traumatic experience, many children do not get the help they desperately need because the adults around them think the children do not yet understand what has happened and therefore do not require such care.

Also, research describing how often kids experience different types of trauma is very hard to come by; such research often suffers from errors in reporting certain traumas such as child abuse, neglect, or sexual assault—traumas that are usually underreported.

For the traumas discussed in previous chapters, rates of natural disasters and crime exposure largely follow the rates found for adults in the community in which the child lives. Children living in higher crime areas are more likely to be the victim of crimes than children living in lower crime areas. Research has shown that people living in large urban inner cities experience traumatic events as much as military service members in combat zones do, and many of these events are witnessed or experienced by children. Kids whose families live in housing that is more susceptible to natural disasters such as poorly maintained housing or temporary housing, and homeless children are more at risk of exposure to negative consequences of the type of trauma we discussed in Chapter 2 of this volume, such as loss of their housing and all their possessions.

The experience of physical or sexual abuse is especially hard for children. In such cases, children are often hurt by those very people who are supposed to be protecting them. The people they should be able to trust betray them by physically hurting them or inappropriately touching them. To add to the violation of trust in the moment, children who experience abuse are often told it is their fault and blamed for the very crime that is being committed against them; they may be told not to tell anyone or they will be judged as bad. Sometimes the perpetrator tells the child that if she tells, her family will be killed or harmed. Such experiences can leave kids feeling ungrounded and unable to feel safe anywhere. You can imagine that having your world shaken this way early in life is especially difficult because you have no safe experience to go back to or remember. The whole world becomes an attacker that is ready to harm you, and you can't trust anyone to protect you.

It is also complicated by the fact that children very often love their abusers, or sometimes report liking the attention even though they don't like what is happening to them. It is important to normalize this for children who have been abused. It is not helpful to say, "How can you love him after what he did to you? He's a monster." Children very often feel protective of their abusers, and it is hard enough for them to disclose abuse without causing them more shame.

How important are caregivers in children's experience of trauma?

For children, the experience of trauma is tied to their caregivers, including parents, guardians, foster parents, or anyone entrusted with the care of the children. Kids have even less control than adults during and after trauma. Children are at the mercy of their caregivers. If the caregivers are supportive, loving, and have resources to help, then the impact of trauma can be reduced. If, on the other hand, the child has caregivers who are overwhelmed, unsupportive, and not able to show love; who are the perpetrators of the trauma; or who do not have resources to help, then the child is especially at risk for negative consequences.

Consider the case of children trapped in countries with political and social upheaval and war. For children experiencing war and upheaval, the experience of trauma is greatly increased as they may experience violence while also experiencing loss of their home and stability, separation from loved ones, witnessing atrocities, and other terrible events. Such children may experience the symptoms of PTSD from exposure to violence or warfare and, at the same time, they may have to find food and shelter. If they are lucky enough to escape this conflict zone and move elsewhere, with the move they may need to learn a new language and culture while feeling isolated and out of place. If their exposure to violence has left these children with PTSD symptoms, that makes life and these transitions even more challenging. These transitions can be difficult for children even in the best of circumstances and are especially hard for those children who survived trauma. Children are an especially vulnerable group, and they often do not have a voice to ask for help.

What about neglect?

Neglect is another type of potentially traumatic event that is specific to children. Neglect occurs when a caregiver is not meeting the food, shelter, and emotional needs of the child. While neglect is harmful in many ways, it may or may not be a trauma as we talked about in Chapter 1 of this volume: For neglect to be considered specifically traumatic as we use that term for the diagnosis of PTSD, it needs to be potentially life-threatening to the child. So not having food to the point of malnourishment may meet that definition. Certainly emotional abuse that includes life threats or bodily threats would meet that definition. What we know about neglect—whether or not it specifically meets the definition of trauma—is that *kids who are neglected are at a much higher risk of exposure to other types of trauma, including physical and sexual abuse and rape.* To make matters even worse, if neglected children experience those other traumas, such children are also at very high risk for developing mental health disorders such as PTSD, depression, and substance abuse. *Consider 10-year-old Destiny who was molested and goes home to parents who tell her that she is worthless and stupid; that child is getting multiple messages from adults confirming that she is not worth anything and not worth protecting. This message sinks in and forms her self-image in a way that can be hard to change as she grows up.* We can think of neglect as the poisoned soil that magnifies any stressful experiences in life. Neglect also changes how our bodies respond to trauma and stress and makes us more vulnerable to problems such as PTSD, depression, and substance abuse.

Jonathan's abusive father

Jonathan grew up in a chaotic household. His father, Michael, was physically abusive to both Jonathan and his mother, Mary. His father often came home angry from work and beat Jonathan with a belt. Not long after Michael finished beating him, Jonathan would hear screaming from his mother in the next room. Jonathan felt helpless to assist his mother, but he still felt ashamed that he didn't help her.

Jonathan's father was abusing stimulants, including cocaine and methamphetamine, and he was often away from home for weeks at a time. Money was scarce due to Michael's drug habit and absences from work. Mary did not work outside the home, and when Michael would disappear, mother and child would have to find ways to make the food stretch until Michael returned. While Jonathan's mom was a loving person, she was not able to protect her son from his father's anger. When Jonathan was 7, his mother died after a particularly brutal attack by her husband. While Jonathan suspected that his father had intentionally tried to kill his mother, he was not able to tell anyone for fear that his father would also try to kill him.

Jonathan remained in the home for 2 years after his mother's death. During this time, the boy often was left alone for a week or more to care for himself. This situation continued until Jonathan's aunt Renee (his mother's sister) took him to live with her. While Renee was loving and supportive and she connected Jonathan to a psychologist who worked with him on his PTSD, it took about 2 years before his aggressive behavior at school decreased. The aunt's firm and constant loving attention helped Jonathan learn new ways to interact with the world, and the exposure therapy he did with the therapist helped reduce the nightmares of the night his mother died. Having a patient and loving adult and a safe home with food and reliable shelter allowed Jonathan to connect with the world in a new way, but his early

life experiences left their mark and made him more susceptible to ex-
periencing PTSD after a brutal attack as an adult.

Does trauma impact schooling?

In the United States, the primary responsibility for most children is school, but when children experience trauma, concentration can be difficult. This is part of the natural recovery
process shortly after trauma exposure. In Chapter 3 of this
volume, we discussed the consequences of trauma exposure
in adults, one being that the trauma memory will pop into the
survivor's awareness in images, nightmares, and thoughts.
For most people who experience trauma, these symptoms
happen for a few weeks and gradually decrease over time.
The same is true for children. You can imagine how difficult
it would be paying attention to your teacher or sitting still in
class to read if you are thinking about when you were attacked
or reliving your mother's screams when she was attacked. If
your teachers and caregivers know about the trauma and understand the natural recovery process, they can be supportive
and helpful. However, if teachers and caregivers are not aware
of what happened, as is often true for children who experience
physical or sexual abuse or rape, teachers may interpret this
as bad behavior or attention issues. If a child's school performance changes significantly in a short period of time, talking
with her about whether anything has changed in her life and
gentle discussion to determine if trauma has occurred may
help to provide an opening for the child to disclose abuse or
neglect. Adults at school are often the best chance that children
in an abusive environment have to let people know they are
being hurt at home. Watching for signs of abuse and neglect is
an important function of our school system. Almost all states
have mandatory reporting laws requiring professionals to report child maltreatment. Individuals designated as mandatory
reporters typically have frequent contact with children. Such
individuals may include social workers; teachers, principals,

and other school personnel; doctors, nurses, and other health-care workers; counselors, therapists, and other mental health professionals; child care providers; medical examiners or coroners; and law enforcement officers.

As already discussed, Jonathan's childhood home environment was neglectful and abusive. His family had been reported to social services many times, but each time the social worker would stop by, Jonathan's father would straighten up for a few days, clean the house, and make sure things looked right for the social worker's return. He would stop his abusive attacks and promise never to do them again. This would typically last a few months and then start over. Jonathan was placed in the special needs class and often got in trouble for fighting at school. Looking back, adult Jonathan said that he felt like he was constantly ready to explode during that time in his life. He often fantasized about running away. When he started going to a new school after moving in with his aunt, he continued to have problems with managing his anger and had several fights at school. However, since his aunt was open with school officials about Jonathan's past, they were able to set up a plan. As he worked with a therapist on his trauma and connected with his aunt as a loving caregiver, his anger subsided, and he stopped acting out and fighting.

Do children get depressed or have PTSD after trauma?

In Chapter 1 of this volume, we discussed reactions that people can have after trauma and the natural recovery process. All of what we described for adults is true for kids as well. Most children who experience trauma go on to recover and function well over their lives, but a significant minority may develop PTSD, depression, and/or another mental health issue. Early childhood trauma, especially when it is repeated or combined with caregiver neglect, can result in problems getting along with others; such problems are often diagnosed as personality disorders or disorders of attachment. These problems make sense since children who learn early that other people do not take care of them, that the world is out to take advantage of them, or even that they are only valuable for their looks or their bodies will have problems in relationships and social functioning as they grow up. It may be difficult to trust people and feel the normal closeness to others. Children are more likely to have mental health issues or problems with social functioning when they do not have stable, loving caregivers who can support the child feeling safe following trauma.

For Jonathan, the 2 years he spent in the home with his father after his mother's death were the worst. He felt totally isolated and blamed himself for not protecting his mother. His father, Michael, was especially physically and emotionally abusive during those years, often leaving Jonathan with large bruises from his belt on Jonathan's back. During that time, Jonathan was haunted by his mother's screams, and her words to him that night to just sit still and be quiet until his father was done. He could see her bruised face when he closed his eyes. Whenever he tried to read, the images popped back in his mind's eye. He couldn't sleep and regularly stayed up all night just watching TV until he nodded off for an hour or so and then awakened, startled, by the smallest sound in the apartment. He felt worthless, and his father made sure he felt helpless and hopeless with his continued emotional and physical abuse. Jonathan did not know any of his relatives; Michael had kept Jonathan and his mother totally isolated from the rest of the family, and the boy felt completely alone and isolated. He often thought about suicide and considered overdosing on his father's cocaine.

In many ways, the reactions of kids following trauma parallel the reactions of adults with the addition that caregiver reactions can significantly worsen or improve the mental health outcomes for children who experience trauma.

How are trauma reactions different in children?

As previously mentioned, one way that children's reactions to trauma are different is that kids are highly dependent on the reactions of the caregiving adults in their lives. If those adults respond to trauma with support and love and if the resources are there to provide stability, children will typically follow a course of natural recovery over time. If, however, the caregiver responds with any sense of denying the child's experience or by blaming the child, or if resources are not available or if the caregiver is emotionally or physically unavailable, the child is at a higher risk of developing mental health problems over time. Children look to adults for guidance as to how the child should respond. If adults are overwhelmed and very upset, very often the children will be, too. If the adult is calm, reassuring, and trying to maintain stability, that will help the child's reactions tremendously.

For children younger than age 6, the fifth edition of the American Psychiatric Association's *Diagnostic and Statistical Manual of Mental Disorders* has special (different) criteria for diagnosing PTSD—criteria different from those for children and adults over the age of 6. The first difference involves how the trauma is specified. In addition to the way that trauma is defined for adults and older children, if a child younger than 6 has a caregiver who is exposed to trauma, this is considered indirect exposure that can lead to PTSD. Since the reactions of kids, especially very young ones, are tied to their caregivers, this addition makes a lot of sense. As for intrusive symptoms, very young children may express the trauma in reenacting it in play. For instance, a child who has been sexually or physically abused may make her dolls "engage" in sexual activity, or the child herself may engage in precocious sexual activity with peers or she may masturbate in public. Adults who notice such play should ensure that appropriate adults are told and assessment of the child's situation may then occur. Careful questioning to try to find the perpetrator may be necessary. If a caregiver is suspected, assessment for safety of the child may be necessary. In any case, if a child reports physical or sexual abuse or neglect, this information should be reported to social services; as mentioned earlier, this reporting is required for most professionals who engage with children, including psychologists, medical professionals, and teachers.

Another important difference between children and adults in how they react to trauma involves the child's developmental stage and understanding of the trauma itself. Since children may be at very different levels of cognitive and emotional development at the time of the trauma (based both on their actual age and stage of development), their reactions may be dependent on that stage, and their understanding of the trauma may be determined by their developmental understanding.

Jonathan is a good example of this. Since he was 7 when his mother died, he was not able to consider the larger world or the possibility that things could be different. His experience was all he knew, and as far as he knew, all fathers were angry, abused drugs, and beat their kids and wives. Jonathan was not able to imagine a father who was not angry. When his father told him that Jonathan was to blame for his mother's death, Jonathan believed him. If he had been several years older or had been less isolated, Jonathan may have been able to think differently about the situation and see that the blame was not his to take.

In another example, let's look at an even younger child, Hannah, who was 5 years old when her family was displaced due a wildfire that killed many people and burned her home to the ground. Thankfully, her parents evacuated the family early, and Hannah did not see the home on fire. However, her whole world was lost. All her toys and clothes and even her bedroom were gone. Her parents did not bring Hannah to see the burned home, and they did not talk to her about what had happened. Her parents were distraught over the fire and spent lots of time talking behind closed doors about what had happened. Hannah could hear them talking and sensed the anxiety, but they never spoke with her about the fire. They simply said that they were moving to a new place and getting new stuff. As a result, Hannah made up a story about a wizard who took their home and made them move. Two months after the fire, Hannah's mom noticed that the girl was constantly watching the sky and looking very anxious. She sat down to talk with her young daughter and discovered Hannah's story. As a result, the whole family gathered to talk with

Hannah about what she thought had happened and what really did happen, on a level that the young child could understand. Hannah was upset, but now she was able to fit the experience into her life story in a way that reflected her new reality—that wildfires can happen and they are devastating when they do, but my family will protect me and take care of me.

What should we do after a child has been exposed to a traumatic event?

You will see a single consistent message in this chapter on childhood trauma. Children look to adults to offer them security and predictability and even more so following a traumatic event. The most important thing we can do for children after trauma is help them feel safe and protected and to help maintain their normal life routines as much as possible. *To illustrate, 5-year-old Luis slept with a thumb tack under his pillow. He kept the thumb tack as a weapon to protect his mother after witnessing her attack at a train station. His mother had not spoken with him after the attack even though the boy was present at the time of the incident. She thought as long as he did not say anything and was not having problems at school, she would just move on. When she discovered the tack under his pillow, however, their conversation revealed that Luis was scared that his mother would be attacked again. A 5-year-old needs to feel protected rather than feeling that someone is depending on him for protection. His mother let him know that she is safe and will keep him safe. He does not need to worry about protecting her. Adults need to ensure that children feel safe, protected, and understood to the extent that the child is able to understand.*

Another way to support children following trauma is to validate their experience. Let them know that what they experienced was difficult and that it is OK to have feelings and thoughts and even images that may come back over time. Talking through their understanding of the event and what it says about them and the world can help kids feel heard and understood. Let them know that you will do all that you can to keep them safe in the future and always remind them that what happened was not their fault.

Maintaining connection with primary caregivers is important whenever possible. Sometimes in the upheaval of trauma, parents have to separate from children to address work or home needs (find a new place to live, move to new job, etc.). Minimizing such separation is typically helpful to long-term adjustment of children following trauma. If separation is required, making sure the child is comfortable with the temporary caregivers can minimize the impact. Maintaining as much contact with the parents as possible, including long distance face-to-face time such as Skype or Facetime, is very helpful. During World War II, British authorities moved many of the children who lived in London away from the city to protect them from the bombings. It turns out that the children who stayed in London and experienced the bombings but who weren't separated from their parents fared better than the kids who were "protected." The sense of safety that comes from being with primary caregivers actually made a bigger impact on functioning over time than the exposure to the bombings.

Are there treatments for children with PTSD?

In Chapter 4 of this volume, we described several evidence based treatments for PTSD in adults. Unfortunately, we don't have as many high-quality studies focusing on the treatment of PTSD in children and adolescents. As a result, most professionals looking at PTSD in children and adolescents are encouraged to first ensure as much as possible the safety of the child. Once safety is established, it is important to provide education appropriate for the age of the child as well as education for caregivers to understand the child's current reactions as well as future issues that children who experience trauma and develop PTSD may experience.

The best evidence to date for helping children and adolescents with PTSD comes from treatments that are similar to PTSD treatments for adults. These include exposure-focused treatments that provide safe ways for children to approach their trauma memories and learn (a) that what may have been dangerous in the past is no longer a danger and (b) that they can handle it when bad things happen. In addition to these two messages that are critical to treatment of PTSD in children and adults, treatment of children also focuses on helping them learn that kids can rely on adults to help keep them safe.

Exposure-based treatments for children often include play therapy. This tool allows children a place to express their previous experience and how they are feeling about that experience in a nonthreatening manner. This can be especially important for children who have been threatened by their attacker or who do not really understand what has happened. Through play, children can express their experience without having to accuse and risk additional harm or invalidation. Skilled play therapists are able to focus on the child and difficult experiences and help them to approach their memories and work through the feelings associated with the memories through play. For those children who experienced sexual or physical assault, anatomically correct dolls can be used so that such child survivors can easily point to or show what happened to them since they don't have the words or language to describe sexual activity.

Trauma-focused cognitive behavioral therapy (TF-CBT) is the treatment with the most research supporting that it reduces or remits PTSD in children and adolescents. This specific exposure-based protocol includes working in a developmentally sensitive way to help children approach their trauma memory or memories and to start to do the things that they avoid because they remind him of the trauma. TF-CBT is very flexible for kids with single or multiple traumas and even for those children who also have other mental health issues, such as depression or substance misuse.

How important is it for children to hear repeatedly, "It was not your fault"?

Children experience themselves as the center of their worlds. Therefore, if something bad happens, they often feel it is their fault. We see this when parents get divorced: Young children often feel that if only they had been better, the parent wouldn't have left. With trauma this can be even more harmful. *In the case of Jonathan, he was already feeling that he was to blame for his mother's death when his father piled on more guilt. This guilt fueled the child's depression and sense of wanting to die. Once he moved in with his aunt, however, he heard the opposite message. Every day he would hear his aunt saying what a brave child he was and how sad she was that she did not know about him or the situation that he lived in. She told him that he was absolutely not to blame for his mother's death, for his abuse from his dad, or for his father's drug problem. She said this over and over. Jonathan also heard this message from his therapist as they worked on exposure therapy, and more important, Jonathan started to hear it from himself in listening to his imaginal exposure recordings and hearing what had happened at the time of his mother's death. Hearing this message over and over and then actually going through the memory for himself, Jonathan was able to believe that he was not to blame for his mother's death and in fact his father was to blame. When he truly believed this, Jonathan's PTSD symptoms greatly reduced, and he began to feel like a strong and resilient person who had been through adversity to emerge on the other side.*

In conclusion, many children will experience trauma. Most will emerge as resilient adults but some will continue to have difficulties over their lives. Ensuring that children who experience trauma feel safe and supported and stay connected with their primary caregivers, if those caregivers are supportive, can improve these children's chances for resilience following trauma. Providing safe places for kids to express their feelings and understanding of the trauma can support their adjustment over time. Children cannot hear often enough that what happened was not their fault.

AFTERWORD

A MESSAGE OF HOPE AND RESOURCES

A message of hope

As we have discussed throughout this book, we live in a dangerous world, and, unfortunately, about 70 percent of us may encounter a potentially traumatic event in our lifetime, with many of us experiencing more than one trauma. But the good news is that we are resilient, and fewer than 10 percent of people suffer from posttraumatic stress disorder (PTSD). The rest of the good news is that we have good treatments for PTSD.

Many of our patients were reluctant to get therapy for PTSD because they didn't think anything could help. We can't change what happened to them, so how could anything make it better? What they learned is that, although it is true we can't change the awful thing or things that happened, we can change the PTSD and their reactions to what happened. We can change how they think about what happened and about themselves, other people, and their world. We can change how their bodies react to trauma reminders. We can help them take back their lives from PTSD. There is hope. Treatment works.

How to find a provider

There are several different resources for finding a provider. If you have insurance and want to use an in-network provider, you should go to their website and search for mental health providers. Usually they have specialties listed. If they do list trauma or PTSD as specialties, we recommend you contact them and ask what evidence-based treatments they provide for PTSD.

A few organizations that tend to have a number of providers (typically PhD level psychologists) who provide evidence-based treatments for PTSD include the following:

The International Society for Traumatic Stress Studies
http://www.istss.org/find-a-clinician.aspx
The Associate for Behavioral and Cognitive Therapies
http://www.findcbt.org/FAT/
The Anxiety and Depression Association of America
https://members.adaa.org/page/FATMain
The National Center for PTSD website
Note: even though this website is part of the U.S. Department of Veterans' Affairs, many Veteran Affairs therapists also have a private practice or they may be able to recommend a good trauma provider in the area
https://www.ptsd.va.gov/gethelp/find_therapist.asp
The Center for the Treatment and Study of Anxiety
https://www.med.upenn.edu/ctsa/find_pe_therapist.html

PTSD resources

AboutFace and Make the Connection
https://www.ptsd.va.gov/apps/aboutface/
https://maketheconnection.net/resources#va-resources

AboutFace and Make the Connection are two sites presenting stories of veterans in their own words. The stories present military experiences as well as a wide range of treatment experiences and stories of recovery. The site is intended to provide veterans in search of treatment with information to aid their own treatment decisions and encourage hope and help.

Anxiety and Depression Association of America

https://adaa.org/understanding-anxiety/posttraumatic-stress-disorder-ptsd

The Anxiety and Depression Association of America website includes fact sheets and online information on reactions to trauma, PTSD, and its treatment for people suffering with PTSD and their families as well as professionals who work with trauma survivors and others.

American Psychiatric Association: PTSD

https://www.psychiatry.org/patients-families/ptsd/what-is-ptsd

The American Psychiatric Association PTSD page provides brief informational resources for patients and their families on the disorder, comorbid issues, and treatment options with emphasis on medical options for care.

American Psychological Association: PTSD

https://www.apa.org/topics/ptsd/

The American Psychological Association PTSD page provides brief informational resources for patients and their families on the disorder, comorbid issues, and treatment options including psychotherapy and medication options for treatment. The site includes information on how to choose a provider and support resources for caregivers of people suffering with PTSD.

Mental Health Care on the Military Heath System

http://afterdeployment.dcoe.mil/

The Mental Health Resources on the Military Health System website used to be hosted at AfterDeployment.org but now resides here. This site has a wide variety of psychoeducational and self-help materials for issues that may arise after deployment in military personnel. While the primary focus is on military and Veteran issues, many of the resources are also applicable to other people suffering with PTSD or other issues post-trauma, such as sleep difficulty, anger, or substance use.

National Crisis Line

https://suicidepreventionlifeline.org/
The National Crisis Line is a resource for people in crisis and their families focused on suicide prevention. The website has national resources for various crises that impact trauma survivors and people suffering with PTSD. A telephone service (1-800-273-8255), a text service, and online chat are available to call and talk to a person 24 hours a day.

National Alliance on Mental Illness (NAMI): PTSD

https://www.nami.org/Learn-More/Mental-Health-Conditions/Posttraumatic-Stress-Disorder/Support
The National Alliance on Mental Illness (NAMI) PTSD page covers basic information on the disorder for people suffering with PTSD and their families. In addition, it provides information on community resources for support for patients and their families.

National Center for PTSD

https://www.ptsd.va.gov/index.asp
The National Center for PTSD website has numerous resources for any and all audiences who may be interested in more information on the disorder, its treatment, and related conditions and issues. The site includes informational sheets, patient decision aids, and provider training.

National Child Traumatic Stress Network

https://www.nctsn.org/

The National Child Traumatic Stress Network provides information on trauma and stress in children, training for providers, psychoeducation for family, and treatment resources.

National Institute of Mental Health: PTSD

https://www.nimh.nih.gov/health/topics/post-traumatic-stress-disorder-ptsd/index.shtml

The National Institute of Mental Health PTSD page has numerous resources for any and all audiences who may be interested in more information on the disorder, its treatment and related conditions and issues. The site includes informational sheets as well as ways to get involved in research.

Trauma-Focused Cognitive Behavioral Therapy (TF-CBT) National Therapist Certification Program

https://tfcbt.org/about-tfcbt/

The TF-CBT Training Program provides training in this first line evidence-based treatment for PTSD for use in children and adolescents with PTSD. The site includes information on the treatment as well as links to find a therapist trained in trauma-focused cognitive behavioral therapy.

Veterans Crisis Line

https://www.veteranscrisisline.net/get-help/local-resources

The Veterans Crisis Line is a resource for veterans and their families in crisis focused on suicide prevention. It is a part of the National Crisis Line specifically targeted to Veterans. The website has national resources for various crises that impact trauma survivors and people suffering with PTSD. In addition, a toll-free number (1-800-273-8255, then press 1) is available to talk to a person 24 hours a day; a text service and online chat are also available.

AFTERWORD IN THE FACE OF THE COVID-19 PANDEMIC

As we are going to press with *PTSD: What Everyone Needs to Know*, we are in the midst of the global COVID-19 pandemic. Today there are 1,237,420 confirmed cases globally, 321,762 in the United States, with over 67,000 deaths to date. We know we are in the thick of it, but we do not know exactly where we are in it. Most of us in the United States know that we have not reached the apex yet.

These are such uncertain and frightening times for everyone. Front line healthcare workers are feeling like they are in a war zone. They are overwhelmed with sick patients, inadequate supplies, no proven treatments, and sick and dying colleagues. Many have described that they feel like they are in the World War I approach to combat: The first wave moves in a line toward the enemy and gets shot down, and the second wave emerges to approach the enemy knowing that they are also likely to be shot down.

Fear and anxiety are normal in the face of the COVID-19 pandemic. We do not want to pathologize this normal fear and anxiety. We hope that people can use their good coping skills to deal with this unprecedented situation. These include eating properly, sleeping properly, exercising, taking breaks to recharge, maintaining social contacts even if they must be at a distance, being compassionate to ourselves and others, and keeping our thinking rational.

There are many who are experiencing excessive fear, anxiety, depression, and feelings of being totally overwhelmed. If people had mental health difficulties prior to this pandemic, we suggest using what worked previously and reaching out to your mental health providers who are likely providing services via telemedicine. It is important to keep the perspective that this will end at some point. We don't know when and we don't know how bad it will be yet. But even with the overwhelming numbers of people falling ill with COVID-19, most people are recovering and surviving and eventually thriving again. Making the decision to trust that it will probably turn out OK for most of us in the end is a healthy decision. Stay present in the moment and do what you need to do. This always includes breathing! When you don't know what to do, breathe and keep putting one foot in front of the other. If you are left with lingering anxiety that is interfering with your current functioning, we hope this book can help if you think it might be PTSD. The same approaches we discuss here should help. For those without PTSD, this book may give you some perspective on what others are feeling. Remember to talk to others about what you are experiencing and get help if you need it.

Although the precautions to slow down the transmission of COVID-19 call for physical distancing, we are all in this together, and we will get through this together. As we are faced with a threat to humanity, it is important to retain our shared humanity, compassion, optimism, and commitment to help. Stay calm and carry on!

Barbara O. Rothbaum
Sheila A. M. Rauch
April 5, 2020

INDEX

Tables, figures and boxes are indicated by *t*, *f* and *b* following the page number

For the benefit of digital users, indexed terms that span two pages (e.g., 52–53) may, on occasion, appear on only one of those pages.

ABC sheets, 115–16
AboutFace, 102–3, 154–55
acquaintance rape, 40–41
Afterdeployment.org, 103, 155–56
alarm, setting, 125
alcohol/drug use
  case studies, 96
  as common reaction, 15,
    32–33, 52, 96
  self-help and, 60–61
  in sleep hygiene, 124
AME Church shooting, 4
American Psychiatric Association:
  PTSD, 155
American Psychological
  Association: PTSD, 155
anger
  as common reaction, 13, 62, 63
  social support and, 23
anniversary reactions, 133
anxiety. *See* depression/anxiety
Anxiety and Depression
  Association of America, 155

attachment disorders, 143–44
avoidance
  as common reaction, 13, 113
  exposure therapy and, 113
  self-help and, 60
  social support and, 23
  stuck points and, 115
  symptoms, 78
  of treatment, 69–70

basic human needs, 37
battered women. *See* intimate
  partner violence (IPV)
behavioral activation, 84–85
behavioral exposures, 72
benzodiazepines, 126–27
booster sessions, 131
burn survivors, 53

Camp Fire (Paradise, CA), 48
CAPS-5, 101
caregivers in experience of
  trauma, 139, 144–45, 146–47

case studies
  alcohol/drug use, 96
  avoidance symptoms, 79
  childhood abuse, 141,
    143–44, 146–47
  combat veterans, 17, 51, 62–63
  early intervention, 70
  flashbacks, 77–78
  follow-up assessments, 73
  hypervigilance, 81–82
  intrusive symptoms, 76–77
  motor vehicle crash, 18
  narrative therapy, 71
  negative mood symptoms, 80
  OCD, 88–89
  overview, 16
  panic disorder, 86
  relationship problems, 99
  sexual assault, 16, 32–33, 41, 62,
    96–97, 100
  social anxiety disorder, 90
  social support, 23, 95
  specific phobia, 91
  treatments for PTSD, 133
CBT-I Coach, 121
childhood abuse
  caregivers in experience of
    trauma, 139, 144–45, 146–47
  case studies, 141,
    143–44, 146–47
  depression and, 143
  foster care system, 46–47
  guilt/blame, 150
  neglect, 140
  PTSD diagnosis, 145
  as PTSD risk factor, 24–25
  reaction to trauma in, 144
  response to, 45
  schooling impacts, 142
  sexual, 138–39, 145
  supportive response to, 147
  trauma impacts on, 137
  trauma prevalence, 137
  treatments for PTSD, 148

  war/conflict zones, 139–40
childhood sexual abuse, 2
chronic grief, PTSD vs., 83
Clinician-Administered PTSD
  Scale, 101
clock watching, 124
clusters of symptoms, 75, 100–1
cognitive behavioral model of
  emotion, 29f, 29, 30f, 31f
cognitive behavioral therapy
  (CBT), 8, 84–85, 106–7,
  126–27
cognitive processing therapy
  (CPT), 8, 115, 126–27
cognitive therapy, 114
combat veterans
  avoidance symptoms, 79–80
  case studies, 17, 51, 62–63
  memory retention, 34
  mental health issues, 24
  posttraumatic growth
    following, 27
  response to, 50–51
  sharing with close friends/
    family, 63
compulsions, 88
COPE protocol, 98
CPT (cognitive processing
  therapy), 8, 115, 126–27
CPT Coach, 120–21

debridement, 53
decompensation, 47–48
depression/anxiety
  CBT, 107
  childhood abuse and, 143
  as common reaction, 14
  exercise benefits, 67
  as symptom, 84
Diagnostic and Statistical Manual
  (DSM), 82
domestic violence. See intimate
  partner violence (IPV)
DSM-5, 82

Effexor (venlafaxine), 126–27
EMDR, 116, 126–27
emotional numbing, 15
emotional processing theory, 25
emotional stressors,
    non-traumatic, 4
ER visit
    IPV survivor, 45
    sexual assault, 39
    treatment in, 71
evidence-based care, 52,
    118, 127–28
exercise, 67, 124
exposure, 126

families of survivors, 57
fear/anxiety, 12, 63
first responders, 3, 48, 99–100
flashbacks, 77–78
fluoxetine (Prozac), 126–27
Foa, Edna, 25
foster care system, 46–47
functioning as indicator, 58

genetic markers, 93
grief, PTSD vs., 83
grief/depression, 14
guilt/shame, 14
gun violence, 2–3

Henry IV, 7–8
high-exposure professions, 3
hyperarousal symptoms, 80
hypervigilance, 81–82

ICD-10, 82
imaginal exposure, 108–11
interpersonal therapy, 84–85
interpersonal violence, 2–3, 43
intimate partner violence (IPV), 43
intrusive symptoms, 76
"in vivo" exposure, 108–11

Kozak, Michael, 25

Las Vegas shooting, 4
life routines standardization, 124

Make the Connection, 103, 154–55
mandatory reporting laws, 142–43
Maslow's hierarchy of
    needs, 37, 47
material support, 54
MDMA, 122
medical support, 55
memory
    erasure, 32
    processing, 35
    retention, 34
    storage alteration, 34
#MeToo movement, 1
Military Health System, 155–56
military service members. See
    combat veterans
mindfulness, 84–85
mobile apps/resources,
    103–4, 119–20
motor vehicle crash
    case studies, 18
    early intervention, 70

NAMI, 102, 156
naps, 125–26
narrative therapy, 71, 115–16
National Center for PTSD,
    104, 156
National Child Traumatic Stress
    Network, 157
National Crisis Line, 156
National Domestic Violence
    Hotline, 44–45
National Institute of Mental
    Health, 102, 157
natural disasters, 3, 47
natural recovery, 26–27
negative emotion cycle drivers,
    30f, 30–32, 31f
negative mood symptoms, 80
nonsexual violence, 2

obsessions, 88
obsessive compulsive disorder
    (OCD), 88, 109
online tools/resources, 102, 120

panic disorder/panic attack,
    86, 109
paroxetine (Paxil), 8,
    121–22, 126–27
partial responders, 132
PCL-5, 101, 127–28
PDS-5, 101
PE (prolonged exposure), 8, 107–
    11, 121, 126–27, 132
PE Coach, 120–21
perpetrator, 2
physical health/chronic pain, 28
physical reactivity, 78
play therapy, 149
police, calling, 38
Posttraumatic Diagnostic Scale for
    DSM-5, 101
posttraumatic growth, 27
posttraumatic stress disorder.
    See PTSD
prolonged exposure (PE), 8, 107–
    11, 121, 126–27, 132
provider, locating, 154
Prozac (fluoxetine), 126–27
PSSI-5, 101
psychological needs, 37
psychotherapy
    MDMA-assisted, 122–23
    providers, 105
    trauma-focused, 33–34, 127–28
PTSD
    avoidance symptoms, 78
    chronic grief vs., 83
    consequences of, 98
    described, 5
    diagnosis, 100
    diagnosis in children, 145
    as disorder of extinction, 6
    genetic factors affecting, 93

    history of, 7
    hyperarousal symptoms, 80
    intrusive symptoms, 76
    long-term problems
        development factors, 5
    medications for, 121
    negative mood symptoms, 80
    prevalence, 101
    risk factors, 94
    subthreshold, 91
    symptoms generally, 75,
        84, 100–1
    traumatic events leading to, 6
    treatments for (see treatments
        for PTSD)
    as war Veterans' disease, 93
    as weakness, 92
PTSD Checklist for DSM-5,
    101, 127–28
PTSD Coach, 103–4
PTSD Symptom Scale
    Interview, 101

rape. See sexual assault
rape exam/kits, 39
reaction to trauma
    in children, 144
    helpful, 56
    mental health issues, 23
    PTSD sufferers, to those who
        love them, 61
    risk factors, 11–12, 21–22
    risk factors/longer term
        problems, 15
    survivors, sharing with close
        friends/family, 63
    unhelpful, 55–56
real-life exposure, 108–11
Red Cross, 54
re-experiencing, 12
relationship problems, 15,
    98–99, 143–44
resiliency, 9, 21
resource support, 55

risk assessment, 15–16
risk factors
    childhood abuse, 24–25
    longer term problems, 15
    negative social support as,
        22, 94–95
    PTSD generally, 94
    reaction to trauma, 11–12, 21–22

safety behaviors, 132
safety needs, 37
SANE nurses, 40
screen time, 125
self-care activities, 72
self-fulfillment needs, 37
self-help, 59
self-image/worldview
        changes, 14, 24
September 11, 2001 attacks, 49
sertraline (Zoloft), 8,
        121–22, 126–27
sexual assault
    case studies, 16, 32–33, 41, 62,
        96–97, 100
    defined, 2
    ER visit, 39
    mental health issues, 24
    police, calling, 38
    PTSD development, 6, 11
    sharing with close friends/
        family, 63
    showering/cleaning up, 38–39
    social support, 42–43
    statistics, 1
    victim blaming, 40
sexual harassment, 2
sexual molestation, 2
sexual trauma, 2
sleep hygiene, 123
sleep problems, 13, 81, 99–100
social anxiety disorder, 89, 109
social support
    case studies, 23, 95
    as coping mechanism, 12, 13–14

first responders, 49–50
    importance of, 37–38, 54
    isolation, 23
    negative as risk factor, 22,
        94–95
    providing, 61
    sexual assault, 42–43
    survivors, sharing with close
        friends/family, 63
specific phobia, 91, 109
SSRIs, 121, 126–27
stigmatization, 49
stimulants, 124
stuck points, 115
substance abuse. *See* alcohol/
        drug use
subthreshold PTSD, 91
survivors, sharing with close
        friends/family, 63
survivor's guilt, 83–84, 114–15

target trauma, 100–1
TF-CBT Training Program, 157
thought patterns effects, 30*f*,
        30–32, 31*f*
tools/resources, 119
trauma
    common reactions to, 12–15
    described, 1
    DSM-5 definition, 61–62
    good advice following, 36
    harmful effects prevention, 29
    military, 3
    people affected by, 4
    prevalence, 4–5
    survivors, common needs
        of, 54–55
    types of, 2
trauma-focused cognitive
        behavioral therapy
        (TF-CBT), 149–50
trauma-focused
        psychotherapies, 33–34
trauma-focused therapies, 106

treatments for PTSD. *See also specific therapies*
anniversary reactions, 133
booster sessions, 131
case studies, 133
children, 148
CPT (cognitive processing therapy), 8, 115, 126–27
discontinuing, 129
early intervention, 70
effects, factors affecting, 32
efficacy assessment, 127
EMDR, 116, 126–27
evidence-based care, 52, 118, 127–28
follow-up assessments, 73
ineffective, 131
memory erasure, 32
memory processing, 35
memory retention, 34
memory storage alteration, 34
narrative therapy, 71
organization ratings, 126
overview, 8
prolonged exposure (PE), 8, 107–11, 121, 126–27, 132
provider, locating, 154
providers, 105
readiness for, 68
sufferer's preference, 127
therapists, benefits of, 111
timing of, 70
tools/resources, 119
types of therapy, 106
Tree of Life Synagogue shooting, 4

venlafaxine (Effexor), 126–27
veterans. *See* combat veterans
Veterans Crisis Line, 157
victim blaming, 40
virtual reality, 113

work problems, 90, 99–100

yoga, 123

Zoloft (sertraline), 8, 121–22, 126–27